2165905

y
913
L99w
Lyttle, Richard B.
Waves across the past

ALLEN COUNTY PUBLIC LIBRARY

FORT WAYNE, INDIANA 46802

You may return this book to any agency, branch,
or bookmobile of the Allen County Public Library

DEMCO

By Richard B. Lyttle

PEOPLE OF THE DAWN
Early Man in the Americas

WAVES ACROSS THE PAST
Adventures in Underwater Archeology

Waves Across the Past

Adventures in Underwater Archeology

RICHARD B. LYTTLE

Waves Across the Past

Adventures in Underwater Archeology

WITH ILLUSTRATIONS BY THE AUTHOR

Atheneum 1981 New York

LIBRARY OF CONGRESS CATALOGING IN PUBLICATION DATA
Lyttle, Richard B.
Waves across the past.

Bibliography: p. 200
Includes index.
SUMMARY: Discusses the development of underwater
exploration which have demonstrated the value of
these archaeological ventures.
1. Underwater archaeology—Juvenile literature.
2. Shipwrecks—Juvenile literature. [1. Underwater
archaeology. 2. Archaeology] I. Title.
CC77.U5L93   930.1   81-5031
ISBN 0-689-30866-3   AACR2

Text and pictures copyright © 1981 by Richard B. Lyttle
All rights reserved
Published simultaneously in Canada by
McClelland & Stewart, Ltd.
Manufactured by Fairfield Graphics,
Fairfield, Pennsylvania
Designed by M. M. Ahern
First Edition

This book is for
BRYCE W. ANDERSON

CONTENTS

I N T R O D U C T I O N

Inventions, many of them perfected in the last few years, have advanced the technology of sea exploration tremendously. In describing the development of underwater archaeology, it has been necessary to stress these inventions and how they contributed to the evolution of a new science.

It must be remembered, however, that no inventions, no technology, and no science would have evolved without the vital, human traits possessed by the brave men and women who venture into the mysterious depths of seas, rivers, and lakes. These traits include stamina, faith, and an abundance of courage. Let's never take such traits for granted.

One other point the reader must remember is that the evolution of underwater archeology has been both recent and rapid. Today, the many excavations in progress throughout the world could fill the pages of several books. The excavations described in this book were selected because of their substantial contribution to the growth of the science. It is my hope that these accounts will spark continued interest in the clues to our past that have been hidden beneath the waves.

PART I

The Mediter- ranean

Chapter One

~~~~~~~~~~~~~~~~~~~~~~~~~~~~~~~~

Gods & Heroes

The wind roared out of the north. Rigging lines hissed. Spray wet the tossing boats to their mast tops.

Across the dark sky, lightning bolts crackled. Thunder boomed.

Deeply worried, Captain Demetrios Kondos squinted against the stinging spray. He could barely hold the *Euterpe* on course, and the *Kalliope,* with many planks badly rotted, could not take many more pounding waves. Captain Kondos yearned for the safety of home, the friendly harbor at Syme, but the island of Syme lay far to the east across the Aegean Sea. The little sponge boats needed immediate shelter.

The sponge season of 1900 was an unlucky one for Kondos and his men. The North African coast where they worked had been lashed repeatedly by storms. Again and again, the boats had been forced to run to port. Then, trying for a full harvest, they had stayed at the sponge grounds too long. So now, homeward-bound at last, they faced more bad luck—a northern storm.

But luck was about to change for the sponge fishermen.

As Captain Kondos stood at the helm with one hand shielding his eyes, a flash of lightning silhouetted a dark shape on the horizon. The captain's shout was lost in the wind, but as soon as he changed course, he waved and pointed to make sure that the *Kalliope* followed his lead.

The captain had sighted Antikythera, a bleak island that stood halfway between Crete and the mainland of Greece. The ships could not reach the port on the north shore, but by sailing to the south they could find a safe anchorage in the lee of Antikythera.

The captain and his men thus repeated a drama that has occurred countlessly in the Mediterranean Sea—a

Bound for their home harbor at Syme, Captain Kondos and his men found shelter behind Antikythera.

sudden storm, a run for cover, and then hours of idleness waiting for calm to return. But this time, there was a difference. The men did not want to be idle.

Soon after the anchor chains clanked out in the quiet water below Antikythera's steep cliffs, Elia Stadiatis, a veteran diver, said that it looked like a good spot for sponges. Captain Kondos was not so sure, but he shrugged. What harm could come of it? They were in safe water, and certainly they could use more sponges in the cargo bin.

After Stadiatis donned the diving suit, his shipmates helped him into the heavy boots and the weighted belt. Captain Kondos warned that the storm might be causing some unusually strong currents. Stadiatis nodded. He would be careful.

His helpers then fastened the bronze helmet over his head, and with the air pump wheezing, the diver dropped over the side to vanish beneath a lace of bubbles.

The first full adventure in underwater archeology had begun.

A bright sun broke through the clouds and sparkled on the waves, but below, the shadows deepened as the diver descended. He passed the forty foot level with no bottom, puzzled that water so close to shore could be so deep. Sixty feet, then ninety feet, and still no bottom.

Finally, at a depth of 140 feet, he landed in soft ooze. The bottom sloped steeply away from the island, and the darkness made it difficult to find a firm foothold. Stadiatis steadied himself with the signal line and waited for his eyes to adjust to the gloom.

Suddenly, he blinked with surprise, stepped back, and almost fell. Staring at him from the blue shadows was the head of a giant horse. For a moment the diver could only stare back in wonder. Were his eyes playing a game with him? Then he looked carefully about, one side, then the other. He gaped in amazement. He stood in a crowd of silent giants.

Some stood upright, waist high in mud. Others had fallen with just an arm or a leg showing above the ooze. Close by, a black hand jutted from the mud. It seemed to be pointing directly at the diver. He gripped it cautiously and pulled. With a swirl of mud, an entire arm came free in Stadiatis's hand.

The diver gave four sharp tugs on the signal line. He had seen enough, an undreamed of wealth in old statues. The number challenged the imagination. Would his shipmates believe the discovery? As he ascended, Stadiatis kept a tight hold on the black arm.

Then, the moment he broke surface, he held it aloft. Eagerly, his shipmates took it from him and pulled him aboard.

"Statues!" Stadiatis gasped as soon as the helmet came off. "Bigger than life, statues everywhere!"

Captain Kondos took the arm and examined it carefully. Though black with age, the arm was made of bronze, a hollow casting, typical of the ancient statues that all sponge divers longed to find. Then the captain turned to the diver and eyed him closely.

Stadiatis was as honest as the next man, but he had just come up from a deep dive, and in the depths, any man can become confused and see strange things. The diver smiled. "It's true," he said with a nod. "Go see for yourself."

Captain Kondos decided he would do just that. Stadiatis climbed out of the suit and the captain got into it, but before the heavy gear went on, he picked up a tape measure. When he went over the side, he was determined to discover exactly what Stadiatis had found.

No time was lost in locating the statues. The captain almost landed on top of one of them. Stadiatis was right. Many statues, depicting gods or giants, lay or stood in the gloom. The black figures were bronze, while those that seemed grayish-blue were actually carved from white limestone. The statues were scattered along a ridge of rubble that Kondos believed marked the remains of a ship. The ridge was 150 feet long and extended down the slope from a depth of 130 feet at one end to 180 feet at the other.

It was almost too deep for safe salvage work, but the treasure was certainly worth some risk.

When the captain returned to the surface, he told his men to get ready to sail at once. True, the wind had barely begun to ease, but there was now important news to carry home to Syme.

There they would be greeted as heroes. Everyone on the island would turn out for the celebration. Indeed, if the proper steps were taken, everyone on the island would soon be rich beyond dreams.

Of course, care must be taken not to let word of the discovery spread. The Greek government, like others around the Mediterranean, now had laws banning the private salvage and sale of ancient art works. Most spongemen ignored the laws whenever they found relics of value. The relics, after all, were made by ancient Greeks. Didn't the Greeks who found them have a just claim? Laws denying a Greek this heritage, Captain Kondos believed, were foolish laws. And yet, the laws carried heavy fines for those who were caught. Matters must be handled with discretion.

Long ago, when the Greeks ruled the Mediterranean World, their statues stood everywhere. Public courtyards and buildings, shrines, and most private homes were adorned with statues. It was a poor household that did not boast at least one image of a favorite deity.

Displaying statues was the accepted way to worship the gods and honor the heroes, and with many gods in the Greek religion and many heroes in its past, the demand for statues never ceased.

Sculptors received good pay and much honor, but they had to keep busy. In the early days of their craft, they carved figures from wood. Then more permanent marble became popular, and finally, when the art of casting was learned from the Egyptians, bronze statues dominated. Casting bronze, even with modern equipment, requires great skill and patience, but the Greek sculptors were masters and evidently tireless.

One famous sculptor produced more than fifteen hundred statues in his lifetime. He was Lysippus, an artist of the Fourth Century B.C. His figures were so lifelike, we are told, that they seemed to have been molded from the living flesh.

When Rome replaced Greece as the dominant force in the Mediterranean world, the demand for statues increased. The Romans, having adopted the Greek gods and customs, wanted to fill their homes and temples with statues. Sculptors could not produce original works fast enough, so copies were made to meet the demand.

Today, our appreciation of some of the greatest sculptors the world has ever known, is based almost entirely on these Roman copies. Of Lysippus's remarkable output, just one original survived. And the originals of other Greek masters are almost as scarce.

The loss of the statues is one of the tragedies of history, due to ignorance and intolerance. The barbarians who invaded Greece and Rome took delight in the wanton destruction of art treasures, and when Christianity became a force, destroying statues became a serious business. To Christians, the statues represented idolatry, a pagan practice that must be wiped out. Marble statues were roasted in ovens to produce lime. Bronze statues were melted down and recast to make bells for churches or cannons and other weapons for warfare.

By the time people realized what was happening, the destruction had been all but finished. Copies, some of them too crude to be of much value, and a very few originals remained. The statues had been virtually erased from the land. But the sea held unknown treasures.

For many centuries, no one suspected that the sea could yield up the cargoes it had claimed. The first hint did not come until late in the eighteenth century when five bronze pieces, including portraits of Sophocles and Homer, were brought up from shallow water off Livorno, Italy.

At the time, the discovery prompted such scant attention that we still don't know how the bronzes were found or recovered. Then, in 1832, about fifty miles to the south near Piombino, an Italian fisherman made a remarkable catch. Snagged in his net was a statue of Apollo, the handsome god of light, healing, music, and poetry. The bronze, standing three feet, nine inches high, is now one of the treasures of the Louvre in Paris. Scholars believe that it is an original work dating back to Archaic Greece, a time prior to 480 B.C.

Undoubtedly other discoveries were never reported. Fishermen, slow to learn the real value of statues, sold any metals they hauled up to the scrap dealers. An old piece of bronze was usually worth a few lire. Later, when fishermen rocognized the statues as works of art, they were more likely to sell the piece to a private dealer who could pay more money than a government-operated museum. And even after governments made private sales of treasures from the sea illegal, statues did not always find their way into museums.

Soon after Captain Kondos and his men anchored their ships in the harbor at Syme, the town leaders called a meeting to discuss the statues found at Antikythera. One merchant who had dealt with private art collectors in the past, said that the discovery Captain Kondos and Stadiatis described was worth at least half a million gold drachmas.

It was a fortune! How soon could salvage begin? Who would take charge of the work? How many ships would be needed? The questions were still flying about the meeting hall when Old Ikonomu got to his feet and waited for silence.

He did not have to wait long; the old man commanded great respect in the community, partly because of his good judgment and wisdom and partly because his son was a scholar—a professor of archeology at the University in Athens.

Ikonomu told his friends to reconsider. Treasure sold privately was never seen in Greece again. Always, it was taken away. This must stop. Statues that were made by ancient artists should remain in Greece where their heirs, today's citizens, could view them and be reminded of the great past.

Statues could not be treated like sponges, olives, or a catch of fish. They were not something one harvested and sold to the highest bidder. Statues were beyond value, and no man, no matter how rich he might be, should be allowed to buy them and take them away. They belonged to the people.

No one spoke for a long time after Ikonomu sat down. The old man had touched their pride, and he had told them what had been in their hearts all along. Finally someone asked what must be done.

Ikonomu rose again. He could see disappointment in many faces, so he said that the royal government paid handsome rewards to those who found treasure. It might not be as much as the finders would realize by selling the statues privately, but it would be money legally earned. And if the salvage operation were run by the government the risk of damaging the treasures would be greatly reduced.

The old man said that the only thing to do was to take the bronze arm to Athens and tell his son and other scholars exactly what had been seen at Antikythera.

So it was that a few days later, Kondos and Stadiatis, with the arm carefully wrapped, sailed to their capital city.

Their report caused a great stir in Athens. They told their story first to the archeologist at the university. Then they repeated it before government officials. There were some who thought the sponge fishermen were exaggerating, but even if there were just a few statues at the site, it was worth investigating.

A large ship, the *Mykale,* was outfitted with powerful hoists and diving equipment, and Kondos was asked for his help. Could his two ships be used, and could he provide divers? The government would pay for all services. Kondos agreed.

In November, 1900, the *Kalliope* and the *Euterpe,* with six of Symes' best divers, joined the *Mykale* off the southern shore of Antikythera. A southern wind made it dangerous for the *Mykale* to work close to shore, but the two small ships, with archeologists and divers crowding their decks, moved to the site and dropped anchor. Diving began at once.

The first man stayed down longer than his allotted

When cleaned, a lump of bronze recovered from the first dive of the expedition turned out to be the head of a "philosopher."

five minutes. Captain Kondos was worried, but the man came up safely, and in his arms he clutched a lump of bronze. All hands helped haul the diver and his prize aboard. And the excited archeologist set to work at once cleaning mud and sea encrustations from the bronze. It was the head of a bearded man. His face showed both quiet calm and wisdom, and he soon became known as the Philosopher of Antikythera. The find was a highly promising beginning. But disappointments were to come.

At the end of the first day, after all six men had completed their dives, the *Kalliope*'s deck was strewn with a mixed collection. There were clay bowls, a bronze sword, and several fragments of marble. The marble, badly eaten by sea creatures and chemical action, gave the expedition its first setback. The fragments were so deformed that one could hardly recognize them as parts of statues.

The next disappointment was the *Mykale*. Too large to work close to shore, she had to be sent back to Athens and the divers had to wait for a smaller salvage ship, the *Syros,* to arrive for the heavy work of hoisting.

Then, after work resumed, the divers had difficulty relocating the concentration of statues that Kondos and Stadiatis had reported. The government officials concluded that the spongemen had, after all, been carried away by their lively imaginations. The officials returned to Athens taking *Syros* with them.

It was a major setback for the expedition, but the divers, encouraged by a few archeologists who stayed behind, continued working. It went slowly. The great depth limited each diver to just two five-minute dives a day. Sometimes it took three full days to raise a single fragment. But as the steady work continued, a new collection of fragments grew, and the bronze fragments looked promising. A report was sent to Athens and the *Syros* returned to pick up the bronzes.

The *Syros* steamed home. The fragments were carried to the National Museum where workers began cleaning and inspecting them. The drama began to unfold. Meanwhile, the divers rested. They doubted that they would be called upon for any further work at Antikythera. They were wrong.

The museum specialists discovered to their delight that the fragments made up a complete statue. And as they slowly joined the parts together, they saw that the statue was a masterpiece.

It was the figure of a youth, an athlete in a remarkably lifelike pose. He was in full stride with one arm raised as if receiving acclaim from the arena after a victory. The figure stood six feet, five inches high. Its eyes, made skillfully of gem stones, stared upon the world with confidence.

Scholars from throughout Europe rushed to view the

treasure. Nearly all of them agreed that the bronze had been cast in the fourth century B.C. during the zenith of Greek sculpting, and some declared that it was an original work of Lysippus himself. The bronze, soon known as the Athlete of Antikythera, was priceless.

Three government ships were dispatched to Antikythera, and the divers, when told of the importance of their discovery, went back to work eagerly. They made solid progress. The original cache of statues was finally located and hoists raised many of the pieces. The arm that Stadiatis had found proved to belong to one of two bronze statues dating from the age of Pericles (495–429 B.C.). Several marble fragments were hauled up from the same spot.

And divers recovered many relics other than statues from the site. A bronze bed decorated with animal heads, a gold earring, glass vessels, bowls and lamps of clay, and pieces of human bone came to light. They all told a story of loss and death, but a lump of encrusted metal with dials on one face and an inner works of wheels and gears remained a mystery for decades.

Inevitably, the divers soon had to go deeper to find relics, and one day, a diver came up complaining of sharp pains in his legs. Suddenly he fell to the deck. His shipmates tried to revive him, but it was no use. He became Antikythera's first victim of the disease that cripples and kills divers. A few days later, two other divers surfaced in pain with stiffened limbs. They never fully recovered from their paralysis.

The tragedies forced a decision. Captain Kondos said that there would be no more diving. The water was simply too deep for safety.

It was agreed. The expedition was over. Kondos and his men, full of pride over their contribution, returned

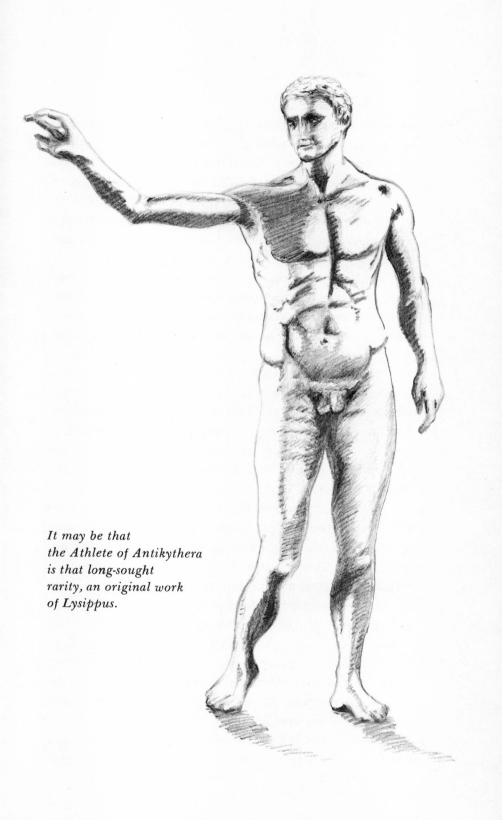

*It may be that
the Athlete of Antikythera
is that long-sought
rarity, an original work
of Lysippus.*

to Syme rich men. Between them they carried one hundred and fifty thousand gold drachmas as their reward from the government. In addition, each diver had been paid fifty thousand gold drachmas. Actually, the royal Greek government, indeed, the entire world, had received a fabulous bargain from the men of Syme. Both art and archeology were made richer by the treasures of Antikythera.

And perhaps more important than all the objects recovered was the expedition itself. It was the first underwater excavation sponsored and organized by a government. And it pointed the way toward further exploration.

In 1907, the French, who were to play a major role in underwater exploration of the Mediterranean, were the first to follow the Greek lead. The French scholar Alfred Merlin, with the aid of the sponge divers who found it, spent six years salvaging relics from a ship that had sunk in the second century B.C. off the coast of Tunisia near the town of Mahdia.

Working at a depth of 120 feet, the helmeted divers discovered that the ship, an unusually large one, carried an entire temple complete with ninety-foot-long columns and capitals, carved ledges, a collection of decorative statues, and even a huge candelabra. Clay lamps of distinct design helped date the wreck.

Fortunately, the columns, carried on the deck, had pressed the statues into the mud, and thus preserved them from much sea corrosion. Close inspection by art experts, however, showed that with few exceptions, most of the statues were copies, some very crudely made. But some true works of art were found.

Perhaps the best of the statues was a smiling cupid that plucked a harp as it seemed to descend from Olympus

on spread wings. A copy, it apparently was modeled on an
original from the fourth century B.C. Scholars, however,
cannot decide if the original was the work of Lysippus or
Praxiteles, another famous fourth century B.C. sculptor.

Although Merlin and his divers salvaged many relics,
they became acutely aware of the limitations of underwater work. And as at Antikythera, some divers suffered
permanent paralysis. Were statues and other relics worth
this tragic price?

There was another serious problem. As yet, no archeologist had donned a diving suit and helmet. All reports
came to the trained experts through the eyes of sponge
divers. And they were not always quick to understand

*Although a copy, the cupid recovered from the wreck off
Mahdia appears to do full justice to the original.*

what to look for or how to salvage relics without damaging them or destroying other relics on the sea floor. So while some treasures came up from the sea, others were lost, and little was learned about the wrecks themselves.

Merlin concluded that the ship off Mahdia had been carrying to Italy a temple that was either purchased or stolen in Greece, but he had little firm evidence to support his theory.

As for the wreck at Antikythera, it was not dated firmly until some sixty years after its discovery, and even then, the dating was made only through an American scholar's curiosity about the mysterious lump of metal brought up from the wreck.

With the help of inscription experts, Derek J. de Solla Price found that when one dial of the machine was set on a date, the other dials showed the rising positions of planets and the moon. The lump had thus been an astronomical device that aided navigation. The machine had a corrective adjustment for leap year, and it was through the corrections that had been made that de Solla Price determined that it had last been adjusted in the year 80 B.C.

This discovery led to the surprising conclusion that many of the statues that the ship carried were relics at the time she sank. But to this day we do not know where the boat came from or where it was bound. Perhaps it was a Roman ship carrying booty from a plundered Greece, but this is no more than a guess.

We do not know how the ship was built or rigged, and we have only Captain Kondos' measurement to give us an idea of its size.

Clearly, if archeologists were to gain knowledge from the sea, more thorough methods and better equipment must be developed.

Chapter Two

~~~~~~

Shadows
in the Sea

On the coast of Lebanon some fifty miles south of the city of Beirut, a cluster of sun-bleached houses stands on the end of a land arm that pokes timidly into the sea. This is Sur, a fishing village of little importance in the modern world.

Brine-caked nets hang drying on the beach, and many of the small boats hauled up there are in need of repair. Even the larger fishing boats anchored behind the small jetty have seen better times. In the heat of the day, the place seems deserted. Sur is a place that the average traveler views briefly before quietly moving on.

But Father Antoine Poidebard was not an average traveler. When he first viewed Sur in 1934, he stared in disbelief.

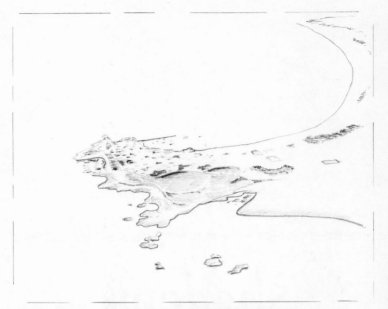

Modern Sur, a small fishing village sleeping in the
Mediterranean sun, gives no hint of grandeur.

The Jesuit priest recalled the description of the place
by the Prophet Ezekiel:

". . . Oh thou that are situated at the entry to the
sea . . . a merchant for the people of many isles . . .
Thy borders are in the midst of the seas, thy builders
have perfected thy beauty. They have made all thy ship
boards of the fir trees of Senir; they have taken the cedars
from Lebanon to make masts for thee . . . all the ships
with their mariners were in thee to occupy thy merchandise . . ."

The biblical passage from Ezekiel goes on to list the
merchandise—silver, iron, tin, lead, brass, agates, emeralds,
purple dye, fine linens, wool, embroidered work, wheat,
honey, oil, balm, horses, mules, and slaves.

Father Poidebard wondered how this tired village
could possibly have been the great Phoenician port of
Tyre. But all the records said it was so. In fact, Father
Poidebard had recently helped erase any doubt about the
matter.

In 1934 he stood both figuratively and actually at the end of a long road. The scholar had devoted most of his adult life to the study of Mediterranean lands. He knew their history and their archeology, and when he was assigned to the post of chaplain in the French army, then occupying Lebanon as a French mandate, he gained the opportunity to explore the old ruins and relics first hand.

The priest's interests had been captured by the Silk Road of the Persians, the overland trade route from the Orient to the shores of the Mediterranean. For hundreds of years, the histories said, mighty caravans had carried spices, gems, silks, and other riches of China and India across deserts and mountains to Lebanon. There the goods were loaded on Phoenician boats for shipment to all markets of the known world.

The Silk Road was abandoned only after sea routes around Africa to the Orient were fully explored and opened little more than three centuries ago. But when Father Poidebard arrived in the Middle East no one knew what route the road had taken. It had vanished under drifting sand and wild vegetation.

He decided to find it. The job might have been impossible if the priest had not been able to enlist the aid of pilots and planes from the French army. He had them fly over the suspected route and take hundreds of aerial photographs. From high above the ground, the photographs showed shadows of embankments, crumbled walls, way stations, and other traces, that had been overlooked at ground level.

Armed with the photos, Father Poidebard then journeyed on muleback to locate and survey the road. He found the ruins of many buildings along the way, including old forts that the Romans had built to protect the caravans from bandits. And he found that the road, the main avenue of eastern trade, led to the insignificant village of Sur.

It was no wonder that he stared in disbelief from the hill above Sur. What had happened to the great port of Tyre? All records said that Tyre had been the principal port of the Phoenicians, and that the Phoenicians once ruled Mediterranean trade.

With stout ships and daring sailors, the Phoenicians had not only made the Mediterranean their province, but they had also sailed beyond the gates of Gibraltar to reach England and to venture down the Atlantic coast of Africa. There is even some evidence that they were the first to venture around Africa into the Indian Ocean.

Their origin can be traced to Syria and Palestine, but many other peoples were also drawn to the narrow strip of land bordered on the east by the mountains of Lebanon and on the west by the shores of the Mediterranean Sea. The Phoenicians thus gained a mixed heritage that combined love of travel and adventure with a keen business sense. These traits found full expression after shipbuilding and navigation skills, probably introduced by the seafaring people of Crete, were mastered by the Phoenician people.

Crete mariners invented the keel boat. A keel not only gave a hull a sturdy central spine, but its fin shape also made it possible to work to windward. Thus the keel was a great improvement over the Egyptians' flat bottomed boats that could not venture out of the Nile without the risk of being driven on shore or simply broken apart by rough water.

The bulk of Egypt's foreign trade was already being handled by the Cretans when they established colonies on the Lebanon coast and taught their skills to the Phoenicians. The Phoenicians learned quickly, soon replacing their masters, expanding the trade contracts with Egypt,

Phoenician ships like the one depicted in this stone carving were among the first to have keels.

and then, in about 1100 B.C., establishing colonies of their own all around the Mediterranean. On the north coast of Africa, one of these colonies, Carthage, was to become Rome's great rival.

In their colonies and their home cities, the Phoenicians built factories to turn raw material into trade goods. The first transparent glass is believed to have been made by Phoenician craftsmen. Glass bowls and bottles, along with pottery, metal work, and textiles brought top prices, but the most precious commodity was a purple dye that the Phoenicians learned to extract from a sea snail that lived in many regions of the Mediterranean. The dye was so highly valued that purple became the symbol of nobility because only nobles could afford it.

Although all Phoenicians shared a common interest

Skillfully shaped glass vessels contributed to the Phoenicians' commercial success.

in shipping and trade, they were never united under a single government. Actually, the port cities along the eastern shore of the Mediterranean were rivals, each trying to outdo the other in wealth, buildings, port facilities, and manufactured goods. Biblos, the oldest Phoenician city, was soon overshadowed by Tyre and its closest rival, Sidon.

So it cannot be said that the Phoenicians passed on a tradition of unifying government to the modern world. But we can thank them for our alphabet. They did not exactly invent the modern system of letters, but they took the best from the East, improved it, and passed it on to the Western world in much the same form that it is used today.

Little wonder that the scholarly Father Poidebard should be fascinated by the Phoenicians and their greatest city.

He restudied the written history of Tyre. He knew that it was not only a thriving port but also a fortress city. It repelled a thirteen-year siege by the army of Nebuchadnezzar II, and it delayed Alexander the Great's lightning-fast conquest of the world by seven months. It would have taken something more powerful than man to reduce Tyre to a humble village.

Herodotus, the father of history, wrote in the fifth century B.C. that Tyre rose upon three islands joined by causeways. And Ezekiel said that the city's "borders are in the midst of the sea."

Herodotus and Ezkiel gave the suggestion for a theory that Father Poidebard believed was worth investigating. If Tyre had been built on low islands in the midst of the sea, then it certainly would have vanished if there had been a sinking of coastal lands. The priest decided to make an underwater search.

His first step, however, was to go back to his friends in the French air force. He hoped that aerial photos would

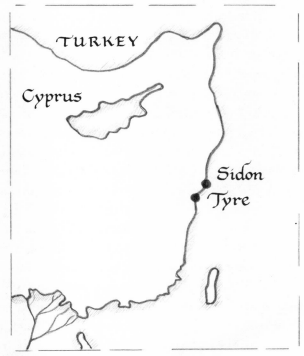

The rival cities of Sidon and Tyre were close neighbors on the eastern shore of the Mediterranean.

pick up shadows of structures under the shallow sea just as readily as they had shown telltale shadows of the Silk Road on the land. He explained his theory to the pilots.

The present village of Sur, he said, very probably stands on one of the three original islands of Tyre. The arm of land that now connects the village to the coast was most likely the artificial causeway built by Alexander the Great's men when they laid siege to Tyre. As for the rest of the ancient port, the priest said that it lay submerged to the north, west, and south of the present village. He asked the airmen to look for signs of buildings and large harbor structures such as breakwaters and jetties.

The pilots, though willing, were a little skeptical. It did not seem possible that waters around Sur concealed a great port. But Father Poidebard had confidence in his theory, and before the air search began, he received strong encouragement from another source.

The French navy was keenly interested in Tyre, not for its archeology, but rather for the engineering secrets it might reveal. The eastern shores of the Mediterranean had long been a problem to modern navies because of silt deposits. Every time a harbor had been built, the silt carried by the coastal currents soon filled it up. Repeated and expensive dredging was necessary to keep any harbor open.

The Phoenicians had no dredges and yet they maintained active harbors for centuries. The French navy, wanting to know how the Phoenicians did it, offered a crew of trained divers to assist in the investigation of Tyre. Father Poidebard accepted the offer with gratitude.

Meanwhile, the pilots and photographers, back from their first flights over Sur, reported excitedly that it was surrounded by patterns of underwater structures. One man said they made the sea look like a Persian carpet. The photos confirmed the reports. They showed the patterns with amazing clarity.

Father Poidebard knew that some of the shadows in the sea could be cast by natural reefs, but the many straight lines and rectangular shapes that appeared in the patterns strongly suggested the work of man.

When a complete set of aerial photos had been collected, Father Poidebard was able to map the patterns and draw up a program for the navy divers. But before the underwater survey could begin, two problems had to be faced.

First of all, Father Poidebard doubted that helmeted divers, slow-moving and always tethered to lines and air hoses, would have the mobility to survey the site thoroughly. He decided to hire a Lebanese sponge diver to work with the Navy men. In the shallow waters off their coast, the Lebanese had always harvested sponges without breathing apparatus. Swimming freely, a well-trained man could dive to a depth of thirty feet and stay down a full minute.

The second problem was not so easy to solve. Father Poidebard, who would be directing operations from the surface, did not like the idea of trusting other eyes with the important work of identifying structures. How could he declare that a structure was man-made if he had no solid evidence to back his opinion?

The answer came from Yves le Pieur, a fellow Frenchman who had recently invented an underwater camera. Father Poidebard decided to make full use of this camera, but he asked the inventor for a change. Give the camera two lenses so it could produce stereoptic pictures. The three dimensional pictures would not only increase realism, but they would also help confirm all measurements taken of the structures.

As it worked out, the Lebanese diver made a greater contribution than was expected. Not only did he lead the helmeted divers to key structures, but he also led them out of trouble when they became disoriented, and prevented tangling and snagging of airhoses and lines. Father Poidebard had no doubt that the free diver's presence prevented serious accidents. This particular diver proved to be an eager worker, always first in the water, searching for promising structures for the navy divers to inspect and photograph.

The first job of the expedition was to identify structures. In some cases erosion and in others the accumulation of silt, mud, and seaweed made the work difficult. The divers carried pickaxes to clear away sea deposits. Often they had to chip for hours at encrustations of shells and minerals to expose the original rock.

Once cleared, the structures were sketched, photographed, and measured. The work went slowly, and the structures proved to be far more extensive than originally supposed. Three years passed before the underwater work was completed. And it took Father Poidebard another two years to prepare his findings for publication.

The ancient port of Tyre, he finally reported, actually consisted of two harbors. The first had been carved out of the sand between the islands and the shore. The second, much larger, stretched away to the south in a complex series of breakwaters, basins, and jetties. In many cases, natural reefs had been incorporated into the structures to make impressive seawalls.

The main seawall that protected the southern harbor was 750 yards long, and storm-scattered rocks at the end of the seawall suggested that its original length may have been even greater. Some boulders in the wall were estimated to weigh more than ten tons.

Father Poidebard found that the seawalls and jetties were arranged so that they funneled the prevailing current through all the major harbor basins. This surprised modern engineers who had been designing harbors to block off the current, but Father Poidebard explained that the current served to flush the basins, keeping them silt free.

The work at Tyre sparked a tremendous interest in ancient, seafaring peoples, and the search for more knowledge about the Phoenicians particularly was taken up with great zeal. One expedition that followed Father Poidebard's seemed to solve a problem that the research at Tyre had been unable to explain. How did a port city built on offshore islands supply itself with fresh water? Water could have been delivered from the mainland in boats, but this source would have been cut off during siege, and Tyre had the ability to survive under siege.

It was the investigation of the remains of a small island community not far from Tyre that suggested the answer. Divers there found that a fresh water spring beneath the sea had been capped and piped to bring water to the surface. Although we cannot be sure that the same system was used at Tyre, the find gave further evidence of the resourcefulness of the Phoenicians.

After World War II, Father Poidebard himself returned to the coast of Lebanon and conducted an extensive diving expedition at Sidon, the rival port some thirty miles north of Tyre. His findings showed that Phoenician engineers had remarkable versatility. Not an island city, Sidon stood on a point of land. The harbor there could not be flushed by directing current through the basins, so the Phoenicians used a different system. They built sluices at the entry to the harbor that sent currents running against the prevailing drift. These counter currents prevented the accumulation of silt in the harbor's basins and channels.

So the puzzle that had been troubling the French navy was fully solved. The Phoenicians used the forces of nature, however they might occur, to keep their harbors open.

Father Poidebard made many other valuable contributions. Because his primary goal was to increase knowledge, he set a new standard for underwater archeology. Certainly, it would have been a happy accident if a sunken cache of statues or other treasures had been recovered from the harbor, but relics by themselves, he said, should not be the sole quest of archeology. They are important only when they contributed to the main quest—our knowledge of the past.

Father Poidebard also showed that underwater archeology should not only be based on solid scholarship but also take full advantage of all available technology. Thanks to support of the French army and navy he was able for the first time to combine aerial photography with a diving operation. He was also the first to use underwater photography for research and the first to recognize the value of underwater stereoptic pictures. And his use of a free-swimming diver pointed the way to the great breakthrough that would expand man's world of underwater exploration.

Chapter Three

~~~~~~~~~~~~~~~~~~~~~~~~~~~~~~~~~~

Challenge
& Debate

When Father Poidebard published his findings on Tyre, archeologists had already begun to take sides in what was to become a long-running debate. The issue simply stated was this: is underwater archeology worth the trouble?

The advocates of the new science, low in number but high in enthusiasm, were quick to point to the advantages of underwater exploration.

Anything found underwater, they said, was almost sure to have escaped tampering by man. The cargo of a shipwreck, for instance, would be found intact, usually just as it had been stowed before the vessel sank. No vandals or robbers would have disturbed it even though it might be many centuries old. The same could rarely be said of land sites where any items of value, even the very stones of buildings, were often removed long before archeologists came on the scene.

Water was a gentle preserver. Metals that might rust away in the air in a few centuries, survived in water. And while wood could be destroyed by marine borers, organic material did not rot underwater at the rapid rate it did in the earth. Furthermore, when wood was covered by silt or imbedded in mud, as often happened with a shipwreck, marine borers could not get to it.

Dating of relics, particularly from a shipwreck, was far more certain than on land. When the date of the sinking was fixed, all items in the wreck were sure to be of the same date or earlier. In fact, a wreck could be regarded as a time capsule preserved beneath the sea.

But the critics of underwater archeology answered with some telling points.

Quite correctly, the critics declared that the many techniques developed for dry land digs, including grids and survey gear for mapping a site and recording the precise location of artifacts, had not yet been used underwater.

The critics also said that leisurely examination of an underwater sight was almost impossible because a diver's time was limited. And divers were so restricted by their heavy gear, there were many things they simply could not do even if they had all the time in the world.

But perhaps the most telling criticism was that no professional archeologist had as yet viewed a sunken ship or submerged ruins. Underwater work had to be done by divers, and because of the special training needed and the risks involved in diving, it was unlikely that any archeologist would ever become an accomplished diver.

Hiring divers to do the work was not only expensive, but it also invited error. You could not, after all, expect someone with no formal training in archeology to recognize the important features of a site.

At first the advocates of underwater archeology could answer these points with little more than faith, a belief that improvements could be made and that new techniques could be developed. But no matter how great their enthusiasm or their faith, the underwater advocates had to admit that they faced serious difficulties.

Without improvements, it seemed that only helmeted divers would ever discover and investigate old wrecks.

These ranged from minor problems such as the refraction of light in water, making things look three times larger than they did in the air, all the way to tragic consequences, the crippling, sometimes fatal disease known as the bends.

The bends was so common among sponge divers that they had a notoriously short life expectancy. And all too often, those who did manage to survive into middle age were cruelly crippled.

For a long time, the cause was a mystery, but as interest in diving increased, particularly among navies of the world, medical researchers found that breathing air under pressure invited trouble. The trouble had a technical name—aeroembolism, which in layman's terms simply means bubbles of gas in the blood.

The culprit proved to be nitrogen, a gas that makes up eighty percent of the air we breathe. Nitrogen is absorbed in the bloodstream just as oxygen is. Normally, most of the oxygen is used by the body while the unneeded nitrogen is exhaled through the lungs along with other waste gases. But when air is pumped to a diver under pressure, a pressure that must be great enough to counter the water pressure at various depths, nitrogen accumulates in the blood faster than the lungs can get rid of it.

The greater the depth and the longer the duration of the dive, the greater the collection of excess nitrogen absorbed in the blood. Except for an odd side effect which will soon be described, the excess gas causes no threat to the diver until he begins to return to the surface. Then, as the pressure of the water on the body diminishes, the excess nitrogen forms bubbles in the blood. If the ascent is rapid, bubbles form quickly. The same principle is at play when bubbles rise in a bottle of soda pop after the stopper is removed.

Bubbles in the blood stream destroy tissue. If the bubbles form in the limbs, they can destroy muscle or nerve tissue and leave the limb paralyzed. If the bubbles form in the heart or the brain, they can cause death.

Obviously, the researchers sought ways to prevent the bubbles from forming, but they also wanted a method of treating the bends when it did occur. The best, but not always sure treatment, it was found, is to seal the stricken diver in a chamber and pump in air until the pressure in the tank matched the maximum pressure of the just-completed dive. If the air tank treatment is given soon enough, there is a good chance that the bubbles will disintegrate as the blood reabsorbs the nitrogen. Then the pressure in the chamber can be reduced very gradually so that the lungs have a chance to expel the gas without any of it reforming as bubbles.

A decompression chamber, as it is called, and its hefty air compressor is, of course, a bulky device to carry on a diving boat, and the treatment does not always work. So the researchers concentrated on prevention, some way to keep any bubbles from forming. The key to prevention proved to be a gradual ascent, one taken in stages that allow the diver to exhale excess nitrogen through the lungs. It seemed simple enough, but working out safe ascent schedules proved difficult because of the many variables involved.

Not only did the time and depth of a dive have to be considered, but the temperature of the water, the physical condition of the diver, and his exertion during the dive also had to be taken into account. Thus the different navies of the world that pioneered the research, worked out different ascent schedules. All of them, however, have a broad margin of safety, aimed at preventing the bends under the most difficult conditions.

A typical ascent schedule for a forty minute dive at a depth of one hundred feet called for a rise to a depth of ten feet in a minimum of one-and-a-half minutes, and then a wait at the ten foot level for fifteen minutes before rising to the surface. For a dive of fifty minutes to a depth of a hundred feet, the typical schedule required a two-minute stop at twenty feet below the surface followed by a twenty-four minute stop at ten feet before rising.

For an extreme dive of 180 feet lasting fifty minutes, the diver must stop every ten feet, beginning at the fifty-foot level with rest periods totalling two hours. Such schedules, of course, put serious restrictions on deep water work, but faithful adherence to the schedules usually worked. And if the bends should strike, the victim still had a chance of being saved by decompression. So the problem, while not completely solved, could now be dealt with well enough for divers to look forward to a normal life expectancy.

But even with the threat of the bends greatly reduced, there were other problems divers had to face. Not the least of these was the side-effect of breathing nitrogen under pressure. Absorbed by the blood, nitrogen acts as an intoxicant. The effect of nitrogen narcosis, as it is called, differs very little from drunkenness. In fact, it has been said that every fifty feet of depth in a dive has the equivalent of one dry martini. In deep water, beginning divers have been known to tug at their air hoses or try to unbuckle their weighted belts. Even veteran divers have forgotten the work plan for a dive and returned to the surface with nothing accomplished.

Another problem was the danger of air embolism which is sure to occur if a diver holds his breath during a rapid ascent. Breath held in the lungs while the external pressure on the body is diminishing will cause the lungs to burst. Divers must learn to overcome the breath-holding instinct as the first step in their training.

Added to the dangers of diving are the dangers of the sea itself. These include sharks, barracuda, poisonous sea snakes, fish with poisonous fins, stinging corals, strong submarine currents, and countless other hazards.

With all these problems, it was understandably difficult for those interested in underwater archeology to keep their faith, but the successful research on the bends gave encouragement, and the advocates looked for further developments that would make diving safer and more productive.

The big breakthrough came during World War II. It was a revolutionary change—scuba.

The initials that form the word stand for Self-Contained Underwater Breathing Apparatus. Researchers experimented with several different types of scuba gear, but all relied on a tank or tanks that could store air under high pressure. By strapping a tank to his back, a diver could carry his own air supply and swim underwater free of dependence on a surface air compressor and free of an air hose and life line.

Today, we tend to take skin diving and scuba gear for granted, but when inventors began working on the equipment, they probed the frontier of a daring concept. Their main problem was water pressure. At sea level, the air or atmospheric pressure is 14.7 pounds per square inch. Our bodies are accustomed to this pressure, and we do not notice it, but water, being much heavier than air, exerts an ever increasing pressure on a diver's body as he descends to the depths. The pressure increases by one atmosphere or 14.7 pounds per square inch with every thirty-three feet of depth. Thus at ninety-nine feet, the pressure on the diver's body equals four atmospheres, one of air and three of water, or 58.8 pounds per square inch.

Because most body tissue is made of fluids—seventy-one percent water—increase in external water pressure has little effect on these tissues, but body organs that contain air, such as the lungs and sinuses, can be crushed by increased external pressure. The only way to counter the water pressure is to make sure the air pressure inside the lungs and sinuses is equal to the pressure of the water. The tanks of scuba gear, built to withstand a ton per square inch, can supply air under the necessary pressure, but the air pressure must be regulated to match the external water pressure exactly.

The need to regulate air pressure to match the water pressure of various depths proved to be the major stumbling block in the development of scuba diving. After struggling with the problem for several months, the French diving enthusiast, Jacques-Yves Cousteau, sought the help of an inventive engineer. Emile Gagnan, a fellow Frenchman, designed an unusual air valve or regulator. It contained a rubber disk that responded to water pressure so that an increase in pressure increased the flow of air from a diver's tank. A hose from the valve led to the diver's mouth, allowing him to breathe air having a pressure that matched the water pressure no matter what the depth of the dive.

Cousteau and Gagnan developed their Aqualung with the vital regulator valve in 1942, and it proved very useful in wartime diving operations. In addition to the tank, regulator and breathing hose, the complete outfit included a glass viewing plate in a face mask that made an airtight fit over the eyes and nose, a tight-fitting suit of insulating rubber or neoprene, flippers for the feet, and a belt with several pockets for weights making it easy to adjust buoyancy for various diving levels.

Optional gear could be added to fit various needs. Most scuba divers now carry a waterproof wristwatch to time their dives and a depth gauge that can also be worn on the wrist. A knife strapped to the lower leg, a flashlight, or a shark stick can be added as necessary.

Other new diving gear was developed during the war. The U.S. Navy's oxygen breather, using tanks of pure oxygen, and a closed breathing system with filters to remove waste gas, left no telltale surface bubbles, and thus had value when working in enemy waters. But the system was limited because prolonged breathing of pure oxygen at depths of more than twenty-five feet produces a poison that can be fatal.

Another system combined the old with the new. A diver with rubber suit and face mask, instead of using a pressure tank for air supply, breathed through a hose connected to a surface air compressor. With this system, the diver could swim freely within the range of the hose, without need of the powerful air pumps necessary to recharge a pressure tank.

All the new systems gave the mobility of free swimming, a great advantage over the bottom-walking, helmeted diver. And scuba diving gear was not only cheaper than a heavy helmet and diving suit but scuba diving could also be done without the large surface support needed for an old-fashioned diving operation.

Scuba gear, however, did not become generally available to the public until after World War II was over, and even then the market for the gear was slow to develop. Even though it simplified diving, training was still necessary to assure safety.

It was not until instruction was offered along with the new gear that the popularity of skin diving began to soar. When it was understood that everyone who could swim, no matter what their age or gender, could with a modest expense and a few hours of training become a diver, a new pastime was born. Spearfishing, underwater photography, and many varieties of marine exploration became common weekend activities. The new gear also opened avenues to serious research. And it seemed that the advocates of underwater archeology could at last answer their critics. All that was needed was a worthy submerged dig that would prove the merits of the new equipment and methods.

Modern underwater equipment includes the "phone booth" which provides a fresh air, rest station and communication with the surface for a working diver.

Chapter Four

The Merchant of Delos

Old Christiani had a secret. And through all his troubles, he had kept it to himself.

But when the navy doctors told him that he would never dive again, Christiani realized it was time to tell someone. Who would it be?

After two days in a decompression chamber, Christiani had spent months in the hospital bed at Toulon. The doctors and everyone else at the French navy's underwater research base had done all they could, but the old diver's legs remained useless. He would be crippled for the rest of his life.

Now, few friends came to see him, and when they did come they usually brought little more than pity—the last thing Christiani wanted. But one visitor was different.

Fréderíc Dumas came to learn. A civilian advisor for the navy divers at the Toulon base, Dumas asked about

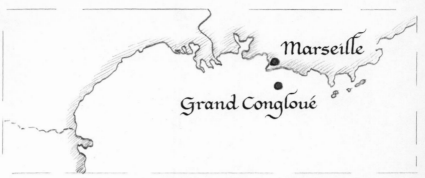

Off the coast of southern France, Grand Congloué lies on the eastern approach to Marseille.

Christiani's years of experience in salvage work, and he asked about the accident.

Without mentioning his secret, Christiani told about his last dive. It was on an October day in 1950 that he went to a depth of 100 feet close to the big rock known as Grand Congloué. Everyone knew the island. It was one of the shipping hazards near the entrance to Marseille, the main port of southern France.

Christiani had stayed down two hours, far too long at that depth, and then he came up too fast. The pain struck at once, and if he had not been rushed quickly into the decompression chamber at Toulon, he probably would have died.

Dumas asked the diver to repeat the story again and again. When did the first hint of trouble come? What exactly were the early sensations of the bends? Had sight, hearing, or other senses been affected? Dumas's regular visits to the hospital brought the two men together. They became friends, and the day eventually came when Christiani told his secret.

It was lobster, the biggest colony of spiny lobster Christiani had ever seen. There were enough to supply the markets at Marseilles for years. That was the reason he had stayed down so long, Christiani explained, he was gathering lobster. They were worth a fortune.

Dumas did not dream of a career harvesting lobster, but he pretended to be interested and asked how to find the spot. It was close to the cliffs at the southeast end of the rock, Christiani said. And it was easy to recognize the spot because the sea floor was covered with clay jugs. The old diver guessed that the mound of jugs provided an ideal shelter for lobster and that explained why such a huge colony had prospered there.

Suddenly, Dumas was genuinely interested. Clay jugs or amphorae meant an ancient shipwreck, and Dumas, a strong advocate of underwater archeology, sensed a discovery. He asked for more details, but Christiani admitted that he had not paid much attention to the jugs. After all, he had seen the amphorae before. Everyone knew that they had been used by the ancients to ship wine, grains, dye stuff, olive oil, and other cargoes, but they had little use now, particularly when broken as most of those he saw had been.

Dumas had a different view, and soon after leaving the hospital, he looked up his friend Cousteau. Now a captain in the French navy, Cousteau had recently taken

Clusters of amphorae—shipping jugs made of clay—are a sure sign of an ancient wreck.

command of the *Calypso,* a ship that the navy had just finished outfitting for marine research.

After hearing of Christiani's find, Cousteau agreed
that there undoubtedly was a wreck worth investigating
at Grand Congloué. Cousteau was just as avid as Dumas
in promoting the science of underwater archeology, and
he particularly wanted to put the Aqualung to full test at
an underwater site. But the *Calypso* was about to sail to
the Persian Gulf on a mission of exploration. Investigation of Christiani's old jugs must wait.

Actually, Cousteau with Commandant Phillippe Tail-
liez and Father Poidebard of Tyre fame had already given
the Aqualung a trial in archeological work in 1948 when
they relocated the wreck off Mahdia. But their time at that
site had been so limited that the results had only been
tantalizing. And in addition to the Aqualung, there was
now another tool that was ready to be tested.

It had several different names—the air lift, the air
pump, the suction pump, the mud sucker, or the vacuum
cleaner. Its design was simple. It consisted of a long tube,
three to four inches in diameter, an air compressor, and an
air hose. The hose was attached at the base of the tube so
that the released air rushed up the tube carrying mud,
silt, sand, and any other lightweight objects to the surface.
Dumas and Cousteau had tested the air pump with good
results, but they had not yet been able to use it for an
archeological investigation. They were eager to start, and
they were not alone.

Interest in shipwrecks along the French Riviera had
been growing with the postwar popularity of skin diving.
By the time the *Calypso* sailed for the Persian Gulf, amateur divers had already located several wrecks in French
waters. And as the number of divers increased, so did the
discoveries. Almost all these wrecks were marked by am-

phora mounds, suggesting that they dated back to Roman times at least.

Many archeologists, including some of those who had not taken underwater work seriously in the past, now began to worry. The coast must be surveyed, the old wrecks located, and steps taken to protect them from theft and vandalism until they could be thoroughly investigated by professionals. The worried archeologists urged government action, and government officials, in turn, brought pressure on the navy to do something about the ever-growing reports of wrecks.

Thus, in August of 1952, the *Calypso* was ordered home.

Her crew of expert divers were to investigate wreck reports, and establish scientific standards for study and excavation. Thanks to the enthusiasm of Cousteau and Dumas, most of the people on the ship looked forward to archeological work and they welcomed the team of specialists aboard. The team was headed by Professor Fernand Benoit, director of the Archeological Museum of Marseille, who suggested that the *Calypso* head for waters off the island of Maire where amateur divers had found a large field of amphorae.

Cousteau agreed, but because Grand Congloué lay close to the route, he asked that the ship stop there briefly to check on Christiani's old jugs. Benoit gave his approval, so soon after leaving Marseille, the *Calypso*'s anchor splashed off the steep, rocky cliffs of Grand Congloué's southeast shore.

Thus began a quest that was to reach twenty-one centuries into the past and lead eventually to a sacred island in the Aegean Sea.

Dumas dove first. The steep cliffs made an overhang that cast dark shadows, but about a hundred feet down, the cliffs ended in a rocky shelf that seemed to ring the island. Christiani had described the place well. Blue and black sea swallows darted through ribbons of brilliant algae. The rocks were covered with sea anemones and dark sponges. At one spot, Dumas came eye to eye with an ugly scorpionfish, but there were no amphorae and no colony of spiny lobster. Dumas returned to the surface wondering if Christiani's memory had betrayed the man.

With time for just one more dive, Cousteau decided to search off a point of rock that jutted from the eastern shore. The dive took him to 180 feet before he reached the rocky shelf. It was strewn with boulders—nothing more. Cousteau swam around to the south side of the point. Again, there was no sign of a wreck. He turned to take a final look at the bottom on the north side. The blue twilight at this depth made it difficult for Cousteau to see clearly, but after just a few swimming strokes, the unmistakable shape of an amphora, sitting upright in the sand, loomed before him. The find was encouraging, but the jug stood alone. It could hardly mark the site of a wreck.

With his diving time almost over, Cousteau edged closer to the overhanging cliff, and there, in the deep shadows, he spotted a mound. It was broad and flat, and as he swam closer he spotted the neck of an amphora surrounded by fragments of other jugs. Quickly, the diver picked up a large fragment and started for the surface. There was just enough air left for a safe ascent.

On the *Calypso,* everyone waited anxiously as the minutes ticked away. When the diver finally appeared, a big cheer went up, and it was answered by Cousteau with a cheer of success. Soon Benoit, with Ferdinand Lellemand and Henri Medan, two others of the archeological team, were avidly examining the fragment. They saw at once that it was not a fragment at all, but rather an encrusted

lump containing three nested cups. Even before the en-
crustrations were completely cleared from the cups, the
experts recognized the unique style. Gleaming with a rich,
black glaze, these cups had been made in the Campanian
region near Naples, Italy, in the second or third century
before Christ.

*Black-glazed Campanian pottery, brought up by Cousteau on
his first dive, helped date the Grand Congloué wreck.*

Benoit asked how soon the divers could begin work.
Cousteau was puzzled. What about Maire? Weren't they
going to look for amphorae there? Benoit shook his head
and explained. Here, off the cliffs of Grand Congloué lay
the remains of what might be the oldest shipwreck yet
known to man.

It did not take long to organize the ship's fifteen
divers into relay shifts, and with the very first dive, relics
began to collect on *Calypso's* deck. They came up in wire
baskets that the divers had no trouble filling. There were
more cups, dishes, pieces of bronze, and amphorae. Some
of the pottery was in fragments, but there were some
unspoiled pieces that looked almost new.

The archeologists worked long hours, cleaning and
sorting the finds, and when each diver had finished his
quota of two dives for the day, he helped with the cleaning

chore. In their excitement, the men of *Calypso* lost all track of time.

Even when a fierce north wind lashed the sea with whitecaps the diving continued. The windstorm brought cold currents to the diving area, but no one complained. The work went on, day after day without rest.

But eventually the relics that could be picked up from the surface of the mound began to give out. Digging with their bare hands, the divers recovered several amphorae, but hundreds of others were held so firmly in hardened mud that they could not be safely lifted. Something had to be done to speed the work. The mound was, after all, a hundred and twenty feet long and thirty-six feet wide. Hand work would take a lifetime.

Cousteau and Dumas decided to put an air pump to work. It meant going back to port to gather the equipment, but *Calypso*'s space by now was so crowded with relics that a return to Marseilles was definitely in order.

Cousteau hoped that a brief stay might solve another problem—money. Months of expensive work lay ahead at Grand Congloué, and the government budget could not spare the funds. Nor could the navy spare the *Calypso* for extended duty at the wreck site. A land base with a small wharf on the narrow beach above the site was needed to cut expenses and free the ship for other assignments. But this meant expensive construction—more money.

The funds would have to come from private donations, and Cousteau knew they could be obtained only after a publicity campaign. News of the find along with the display of relics in the Museum of Archeology should get the campaign started. And indeed it did. In fact, such a large crowd gathered at dockside when the crew began carrying off amphorae, that police asked that unloading be discontinued until after nightfall.

The *Calypso* sailed the next day, right after a new stock of provisions and the parts of the air pump had been stowed aboard. And a few hours later, the ship swung at anchor once again off Grand Congloué while her crew hastened to put the air pump together. As soon as it was lowered into position two men went down to tend the intake. Lellemand took first duty at the upper outlet to clear the catch basket and make sure that no relics were overlooked. Then the compressor was fired up. Immedi-

An air lift was lowered to the site and soon began cutting away the hard mud that held the ship's cargo.

ately, a soupy mixture of mud and foam gushed into the basket.

Suddenly, Lellemand, who was eyeing the mixture closely, jumped back with a startled cry. A large lobster squirmed inside the basket. The archeologist had hardly finished lifting it gingerly from the basket when another appeared, and then another. Happy crewmen hastened to provide a catch box. The evening meal would be a feast.

The best news, however, was that the air pump was performing beyond expectations. It cut through the hardened mud easily, and when the first pair of divers came up from their shift, they reported that amphorae were being exposed in neat rows just as they had been stowed in the hold of the ancient ship. Before long, both crewmen and off-duty divers began hauling amphorae aboard the *Calypso*. The archeologists gave each jug a careful inspection.

The stoppers of the amphorae had disintegrated and the insides were crammed with a strange collection of pebbles, pieces of shell, clay fragments, and in most cases, a live octopus. Apparently the narrow-necked amphorae made perfect havens for octopuses, for when danger threatened they could quickly plug the openings with the refuse they had collected inside.

Many of the amphorae bore the letters SES that had been stamped in the clay when it was still wet. In each case the initials were followed either by the symbol of an anchor or a trident, the traditional weapon of Poseidon, the god of the sea. It would take the archeologists many months to determine the meaning of this stamp.

The ship's radio began to bring encouraging news. Contributions toward the continued work at Grand Congloué were coming in from many sources. In addition to private donations from French citizens, there would be support from the Ministry of Education, the Harbor Ad-

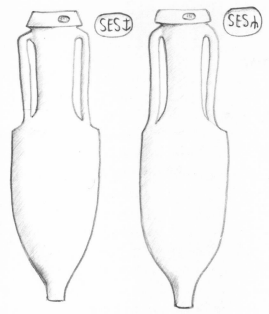

The mark SES followed by an anchor or a trident was to puzzle the amphora specialists.

ministration of Marseille, and many other organizations. Eventually, the National Geographic Society in the United States would make a large donation.

Cousteau was pleased, but he also kept a careful eye on the sky. September had passed, and a storm could strike any day. Anchored close to the rocky coast, *Calypso* lay in a vulnerable position. Without a shore station, work on the wreck might have to be delayed until the following summer.

Luckily, General Marie Eugéne Aimé Molle came to the rescue. As military commander of southern France, the general was interested in the *Calypso*'s work, and he made an inspection call. As soon as he saw the amphorae and other relics and learned the age of the wreck, he promised that the expedition would have its shore station.

Within days of the general's departure, a crew of soldiers landed on the island and went to work. It took the men just three days to build a sturdy platform on the shore, mount a derrick and hoist, and erect a sheet metal barracks large enough to house both the divers and the archeologists.

As soon as the work was finished, the air pump was transferred to the shore base and suspended from the derrick. Waves, which tossed the ship about, had been making it more and more difficult for the divers to hold the air pump in position, but the transfer to the stable base solved this problem completely. Without having to wrestle the air pump, the divers decided that they could now cut a trench through the wreck in much the same way that dry land archeologists cut a test trench to obtain a cross-section view of a mound.

As the trench deepened, it exposed three layers of amphorae, all in neat, upright rows, and from the bottom layers, the divers recovered some amphorae that were still sealed. An overlying layer of mud and refuse had protected the stoppers from decay.

The archeologists gave the seals full attention. The amphorae had been stopped with corks set in pitch and a cement made with volcanic material. Analysis of the material showed that it was pozzolana, a type of volcanic residue found on the slopes of Mount Vesuvius. On well-preserved seals it was possible to read another group of letters—L TITI C F. A quick check with old records showed that there was a prominent family that owned many vineyards near Rome and produced wine under the name of Lucius Titius Caii Fluis. So it seemed that the bulk of the ship's cargo had been traced to its source.

As for the wine itself, it tasted horrible. Cousteau was the first and last to sample the world's oldest wine. His face distorted with the first sip and he spat the stuff out immediately. Sometime during the last twenty-one centuries, the wine had turned sour.

To the surprise of everyone on board, many of the sealed jugs contained seawater. Close examination of these amphorae solved the puzzle. Each had been drilled with a small boring instrument. The archeologists could only conclude that thirsty crewmen of the ancient ship had slipped into the hold to bore and syphon off wine for their own use. This theft, judging by the number of bored jugs, was a common practice, and there were some on the *Calypso* who wondered if drunkenness might have contributed to the disaster that befell the old cargo vessel.

Below the last layer of amphorae, the divers came upon a mixed collection of artifacts—lead weights for fish nets, bronze fish hooks, knives and other bronze objects, including a finger ring. But what excited archeologists more than anything was a large collection of well-preserved Campanian pottery. When cleaned off, the black glaze gleamed like new. No samples previously recovered from land digs were in such fine condition.

Still deeper, the divers found pottery of a different sort—wide, fully curved bowls and vases that suggested the style of Aegean, particularly from Rhodes, Delos, and the Cyclades. And then came another collection of the black Campanian ware, nested bowls and dishes, neatly packed for shipment.

Finally, the air pump came to the remnants of planking, the bottom of the ship's hull. Much of the wood had been destroyed by marine borers, but there were enough pieces intact to reveal some details of ship construction methods of ancient days. Both wooden pegs of oak or olive wood and bronze nails had been used to fasten the planks to the ribs. And where bronze had been used, the shipbuilders had coated each nail with lead. Lead had also been used to sheet the ship's bottom. Such use of lead showed that the ancients knew even in pre-Christian times of the damaging effect of electrolysis. And they knew how to stop this process where the stronger metal in salt water robs substance from the weaker metal. They simply covered all metals with lead to keep salt water from reaching them. Lead also shielded the wood from the toredo, the most destructive of marine boring worms.

Although the trench through the mound gave archeologists clues on the ancient ship's cargo and revealed details of ship construction, years of work remained if the entire mound were to be excavated. And even with the schedule extended to three dives a day, a total of forty-five minutes on the bottom for each man, the work still went slowly. Should the project be dropped? Tragedy almost decided the matter.

Although the schedule tired the divers, there had been no sign of the bends or any other trouble, but then a storm struck and broke a diving float from its moorings. Despite its heavy anchor, the float drifted well into the open sea before it could be recovered. The anchor was gone, but the divers thought they could find it.

Jean Pierre Servanti, a volunteer diver working without pay, suggested that they follow the trail of the anchor where it dragged along the sea bottom. Sure that the trail would lead to the anchor, Servanti was the first to go down.

Unfortunately, the trail led into deep water, and Servanti, probably in youthful enthusiasm, stayed down too long. When his trail of surface bubbles stopped, his friends dove to the rescue. They found Servanti unconscious, one hand resting on the missing anchor. The *Calypso* rushed the stricken man full speed to Marseille. He was hurried into a decompression chamber, but it was no use. After five hours, doctors pronounced the man dead, saying he had probably lost consciousness from overexertion and then suffocated.

Cousteau halted all work. Death was too high a price to pay for relics no matter how old or how well preserved they might be. But there were other volunteer divers eager to take Servanti's place, and the captain eventually decided that the best memorial to the dead man would be to complete the work that he had helped begin.

So diving at Grand Congloué resumed. It continued through the winter and on into the summer of 1953. Work on the wreck was to go on with few interruptions for almost ten years, but in the first two years alone, divers brought up more than 6,000 samples of Campanian ware representing 137 different shapes and styles. It was a bigger collection than ever unearthed from a land dig.

The bottom of the ship yielded two puzzles, a section of lead pipe and a large mound of pebbles. The pipe never has been fully explained, but some experts have suggested that it may have been part of a bilge pump system. The mound of pebbles was explained only after clever, step-by-step detective work by Professor Benoit and a special journey by the *Calypso*.

Benoit's first step, dating the wreck, was relatively easy. The Campanian pottery and the design of the amphorae left little doubt that the ship went down in the second century B.C. The next step, determining where the amphorae had originated, was more difficult. There were two basic types, and the archeologists concluded that one type was made by potters in the eastern Mediterranean, probably on the islands of Rhodes and Cnidus. The second type was made by Italian potters, and because the Italian amphorae lay in tiers above the Rhodes and Cnidus amphora, Benoit decided that the ship had begun its journey in the eastern Mediterranean, stopped in Italy for more cargo and then headed for Marseille, then known as Masilia, the port it never reached.

Next, Benoit turned his attention to the markings on the amphorae—SES followed by an anchor or a trident. The stamp could have been the trademark of a potter, but Benoit thought it was more likely the shipper's mark. The archeologist began a long search through tax records, grave markers, and other documents that had survived.

In the second century B.C., Greek was still the dominant language in the Mediterranean, so it was a little surprising to find Roman lettering on the amphorae, particularly on a cargo that originated in the eastern Mediterranean. But the shipper who used this mark evidently sent his cargo far and wide. Benoit learned that fragments of amphorae, with the same SES mark had been found far up the Rhone valley. This could not be the trademark of a small operation.

Benoit's research eventually led him to a close study of the work of Titus Livy, the Roman historian of the first century A.D., whose writing brought the past to life with detailed accounts of people and places. In Livy, Benoit found his answer.

The historian told of a famous wine merchant, a native of Fragallae near Naples, who became so successful that he acquired a fleet of merchant ships. For a time, he ran his business from Rome, but because of government interference and political uncertainty, he joined a group of merchants who moved to Delos, an island in the Aegean. His name was Marcius Sestius, logically abbreviated SES.

The greeks worshiped Delos as the birthplace of the god Apollo, and the Greeks governed the place with strict rules. No human births or deaths were allowed on the island. Warfare and strife were forbidden. In a turbulent world, Delos was the ideal headquarters for a prosperous shipping village. Livy said that Marcius Sestius built a villa on Holy Delos.

Benoit felt sure he had found his man, the owner of the ship lost on Grand Congloué's rocky cliffs. Cousteau, however, wanted to know more about the merchant of Delos. So, at the first opportunity, he sailed to the island, giving his divers a much needed rest from their labors.

French archeologists began excavations at Delos in 1873, and the work has been going on slowly ever since. Thus, Cousteau and his crew received a warm welcome from fellow Frenchmen soon after the *Calypso* came into the small harbor.

Jean Mercadé, current director of the French excavatons, conducted the men from *Calypso* through the ruins, leading them to what had been the island's Roman quarter.

Livy had written that Sestius built a villa with a large colonnade, and it did not take long to locate ruins that matched the description. Eagerly, the divers began searching for clues. Soon one of the men shouted. The others rushed up and found him looking down on a floor decorated with a mosaic. The design showed a porpoise curled around an anchor much like the anchor in the trademark. Then, in another room of the ruins, the searchers discovered a floor decorated with a trident. A ribbon streamed from each of the three points of the trident, and on each ribbon was a Roman letter, giving the familiar SES of the amphorae.

There was another clue in the mosaic designs, but it was not noticed until Cousteau ventured into an uncompleted portion of the villa and found a spot where the floor was half finished. The captain picked up one of several loose mosaic tiles. It was a black, volcanic pebble, just like those the old ship carried deep in her hold.

There could be no doubt now. The *Calypso*'s men stood in the home of the rich wine merchant, the man who owned the ship they had spent so many months excavating.

So Cousteau and his men had good cause to return to French waters in triumph. They had proven that scuba gear and the new diving techniques allowed the systematic investigation of a shipwreck. They had established the air lift as a valuable tool for underwater archeology. They had raised a variety of relics and even part of the planking from the oldest ship yet known. And they had tracked the owner of that ship to his home.

But long before the work at Grand Congloué was finally completed in 1960, the work there had become a hub of controversy among archeologists. Critics pointed to many mistakes. Perhaps the most serious of these was the failure to map the wreck and locate artifacts before they were moved. So when it was discovered that the amphorae that originated in Rhodes and Cnidus was seventy years older than the amphorae loaded in Italy, some archeologists declared that two ships must have gone down seventy years apart at Grand Congloué, the hulk of the second settling on top of the first. All of the divers who took part in the excavation declared that there was just one wreck, but without mapping of successive layers of cargo during the excavation, it was impossible to disprove the two-wreck theory.

Use of the air lift also came under fire. Digging directly into a wreck with the lift not only risked damage and loss of relics spewed up the tube, but also destroyed the record on the position of that relic in relation to surrounding objects. It would be better, the critics said, to use the air lift only to remove silt or mud from around a wreck, and limit clearing of cargo and hull to handwork alone.

At first Cousteau and his divers, many of whom had

worked with little or no pay, defended their methods fiercely, but today it is generally agreed that mistakes were made. They are rarely repeated by modern underwater excavators. Today, no diver on a respectable archeological dig would think of cutting into the remains of a wreck with the air pump. And no diver will remove a relic until it first has been surveyed, located on a map, and photographed.

Thus it can be said that the experience at Grand Congloué, with its successes and its mistakes, was a vital part of the learning experience. It opened the way for the development of underwater archeology as a true science.

Chapter Five

~~~~~~

Bound for Troy

She was hardly a cruise ship. With a great block of space taken up by diving gear, including a bulky air compressor, accommodations on the thirty-eight-foot sailboat would obviously be cramped. And on this trip, the *Mandalinci,* in addition to her crew of six, would be carrying two passengers.

Peter Throckmorton from the United States and his new friend Mustafa Kapkin, a native of Turkey, inspected the sponge boat with misgivings. Had they been wise in accepting the captain's invitation to cruise a full month aboard this little ship?

Her ballast was nothing more than a loose layer of beach pebbles heaped on the bottom planks. Her engine was an ancient, one-cylinder diesel that had to be started with a blowtorch. Her cook stove was the half section of an oil barrel lashed down at the stern. But the most curious feature of all was her water tank, an amphora strapped to the foot of the mast.

Captain Kemâl Aras explained with a shrug that the

old clay jug kept water fresher than any modern metal
tank, and for sponge fishermen, jugs were easily found
and cost nothing. All one had to do was pull one up from
the sea floor.

The guests' misgivings began to fade. The captain
seemed to be practical and experienced, his crew confident,
and his boat, though weathered, looked solid and sea-
worthy. In fact, she had a certain jauntiness about her.

Throckmorton and Kapkin began loading their gear
on the *Mandalinci*. Grim days might lie ahead but if

A typical Turkish sponge boat, the Mandalinci *was not
designed for pleasure cruising.*

Captain Aras could show them just half the wrecks he had promised, any discomforts would be justified.

Of course, the Aqualungs, tanks, neoprene suits, fins, and masks that the guests loaded aboard prompted a skeptical smile from the captain and an exchange of knowing glances among his men. Captain Aras had already given his opinion of this new diving gear. Playthings for tourists, he had called them. But he had to admit that these two men were quite different from the usual tourists who appeared on the Turkish coast.

Throckmorton, a photographer by profession, had been a salvage diver in the Pacific, a newspaper reporter, and a war correspondent in Korea. He had traveled in India, and in 1958 he had arrived in Turkey in an old jeep that he had driven all the way from Afghanistan.

In a museum at Izmir (Smyrna), Turkey's major Aegean port, Throckmorton had come upon a statue of Demeter, a fourth century B.C. bronze that had been discovered by a sponge diver. And in Izmir, the American met members of a diving club who had investigated several wrecks with the hope that more Grecian statues could be found.

Throckmorton, whose interest in archeology matched his interest in diving, thought it would be a fine idea to try to locate the diver who had found the Demeter statue and persuade the man to show where the discovery had been made. Kapkin, one of the diving club's most enthusiastic members and, like Throckmorton, a professional photographer, thought this a splendid idea and agreed to help.

The two were soon driving south to Bodrum, the main port of Turkish sponge divers. The man they were seeking, Kapkin explained, was a legend. He was known as Amca Ahmed Seytan, actually a nickname which trans-

A statue of Demeter, on display in an Izmir museum, sparked Throckmorton's interest in Turkish wrecks.

lated "Uncle Devil Ahmed"—devil because he had lived into his fifties, a rare age for a diver, and he had escaped so often from storm, shipwreck, and other narrow scrapes that he seemed to have supernatural power.

Past efforts by archeologists to locate Seytan had been frustrated because the man always seemed to be at sea. But now, the two amateur archeologists were in luck.

In Bodrum, they went at once to a cafe that was the gathering place for sponge divers between voyages. Before they finished their meal they were in conversation with

Captain Aras, a tough, broad-shouldered Turk, who thought the strangers were a little crazy and made no secret of it.

Of course there were wrecks, many wrecks, but they had little value. An old jug, if not broken, could be put to use, but what did anyone want with rotten timbers and rusted metal?

And as for this man Seytan, of course he could be found. Wasn't he in Bodrum this very day, waiting to sail on the *Mandalinci*, the ship commanded by himself, Captain Aras?

Eagerly, Throckmorton and Kapkin asked about statues. The captain shook his head. No, he knew of no other statues, but in a month's voyage he could show the strangers more wrecks than they could count on the fingers of both hands. If the two men needed proof, they could load their "playthings" on his ship and be at sea in the morning.

It was a chance not to be missed.

The next day, with her hold crammed with provisions and her deck crowded with eight men, the *Mandalinci* chugged out of Bodrum harbor. Before long, her mainsail caught a fresh morning breeze and the boat picked up speed, plowing through the Aegean's sparkling waves. The boat sailed with surprising ease. Throckmorton and Kapkin exchanged smiles. Here was a promising start for their adventure.

They soon became acquainted with the crew. Seytan, of course, was the veteran, but Ciasim Arslan, the first mate, had also been diving for many years. Ali Zorlu, a young diver, and two ship's boys, fourteen and fifteen, completed the crew. Throckmorton, noticing that Seytan walked with a limp, learned that his legendary powers had not prevented a painful encounter with the bends.

The search for wrecks led from Yassi Ada to Cape Gelidonya with one exciting discovery after another.

After two hours of brisk sailing up the coast from Bodrum, the *Mandalinci* arrived at Yassi Ada, a low, off-shore island. It was their first stop. Soon after he ordered the sail down and the anchor set, Captain Aras explained to the skin divers that seaward from the island stretched a shallow reef that had claimed many ships.

Arslan began to climb into the ship's only diving suit. Soon, with the air compressor chugging, the helmeted diver slipped over the side. Arslan knew the area well, and just a few minutes passed before a tug came on the signal line. He had located a wreck. The water here was shallow, and Throckmorton and Kapkin needed only face masks and snorkels to investigate. They found the veteran diver standing on a heap of jugs and jug fragments. After just a few turns over the area, the skin divers surfaced, babbling excitedly. Below lay a whole field of amphorae, the cargo of a large wreck that was certainly worth further investigation.

But after ordering Arslan to come up, Captain Aras
gave his guests a broad smile. This, he told them was just
the beginning. And indeed, before that first day ended,
Throckmorton and Kapkin had been shown a half-dozen
wrecks. In the days that followed, while the Turkish divers
collected sponges, the skin divers scouted other wrecks in
the area. They kept notes, took photos of all their finds,
and plotted the position of each wreck on a chart. When
Mandalinci finally headed for other waters, the chart
showed the location of fifteen wrecks at Yassi Ada. Some
of them had sunk close to the reef in shallow water while
others apparently had drifted half afloat for a hundred
yards or so before they settled in depths of one hundred
feet and more.

The waters of Yassi Ada held an archeological treasure house, and as Throckmorton and Kapkin saw the
island disappear below the horizon, they promised each
other that they would return. The ship worked along the
coast, seeking good sponge grounds. When a helmeted
diver went down, the skin divers usually donned their
suits and scuba gear. Sometimes they helped the Turkish diver fill his catch bag with sponges or else they took
their spears and hunted grouper or lobster for the evening
meal. If there was a wreck in the vicinity, however, Captain Aras made sure that his guests had time to investigate
it and take their photos. Sometimes fishermen from other
boats in the vicinity would give the captain tips about
other wrecks, and he was usually able to give Throckmorton and Kapkin a chance to investigate these reports.

The *Mandalinci* proved to be a happy ship. The days
were full and satisfying, and the evenings of story-telling
on the foredeck of the ship or around a campfire on the
beach were as pleasant as Throckmorton could remember.
With each day, friendship between the skin divers and

the spongemen grew stronger. Thus, when the voyage ended, it was difficult to say goodbye. Captain Aras insisted that Kapkin and Throckmorton have their first meal ashore at his home. Another captain, a friend from Istanbul who knew about many other wrecks, would be there. The skin divers accepted the invitation eagerly.

The evening turned into a long one, and Throckmorton, having trouble understanding many of the Turkish words and phrases began to doze. The two captains had been talking about the use of dynamite in underwater salvage, when Throckmorton woke with a start. Had someone said *bakir,* the Turkish word for bronze?

Yes, Kapkin explained. Last season Captain Aras had found some pieces of flat bronze stuck to the rocks at a place down the coast called Cape Gelidonya. There was much metal, but the few pieces that they managed to pry loose were so badly corroded that the scrap dealer paid next to nothing for them.

In his drowsy state, Throckmorton dismissed the story. He thought Captain Aras and his friend must be talking about a recent shipwreck, but when he returned to his hotel room that night, he could not sleep. Under normal conditions it took centuries for bronze to corrode, and this bronze, according to the story, was so badly corroded it was stuck to the rocks. Also, the bronze was in flat sheets not in brick shape like modern ingots. Throckmorton remembered reading a book that told of ancient people of the Aegean using flat ingots of bronze for trade. Next morning he located the book among his collection. It carried the reproduction of an Egyptian tomb painting that showed seafarers offering bronze in tribute to the Pharaoh, and the bronze was in flat sheets shaped like oxhides with a "leg" extending from each corner of the rectangular sheet.

Throckmorton hurried off to find Captain Aras, but he soon learned that his friend had already put to sea on another sponge-hunting voyage.

Months passed before he was able to talk to the men of the *Mandalinci* again, but they remembered Cape Gelidonya. Seytan had brought up three pieces of bronze. One looked like a sword, another like a knife, and the third like a spear point, but all were too corroded to be of any value. Another diver remembered finding two bronze boxes full of black, greasy stuff. The diver threw them back into the sea. Certainly such things had no value.

Throckmorton was beside himself. How could he make these men understand the importance of ancient relics from the sea?

Captain Aras, trying to calm his friend, promised to save some pieces of bronze from the wreck after he carried out his plan to dynamite the bronze free from the rocks. Throckmorton was shocked. He made Captain Aras promise not to disturb the wreck in any way until experts had been given the chance to examine it.

But finding experts to take an interest proved difficult. Throckmorton sent off many letters to friends in the United States, describing what the spongemen had found. Finally he received an encouraging response. An archeologist referred Throckmorton to Drayton Cochran, a New York yachtsman who owned a motor ketch and whose son, John Cochran, happened to be an ardent skin diver. Eventually the Cochrans agreed to investigate the wrecks on the Turkish coast during the summer of 1959.

Preparations were made quickly. In June, the motor ketch, *Little Vigilant,* put in at Piraeus, the port of Athens. There she was outfitted for the expedition. Joining young Cochran were three diving friends, Susan Phips, John Richter, and Stan Waterman, who was also an underwater photographer. Although they would investigate as many wrecks as possible, Throckmorton made clear that his main interest was in the wreck at Cape Gelidonya.

With this understanding, and with the air compressor, decompression chamber, and other diving gear loaded aboard, *Little Vigilant* crossed the Aegean to Izmir where Kapkin waited with Rasim Divanli, another skin diver, and Hakki Gültekin, a Turkish archeologist. Director of the Archeological Museum at Izmir, Gültekin had agreed to spend his vacation with the *Little Vigilant* and her crew.

A motor ketch owned by a New York yachtsman, the Little Vigilant *proved to be a practical work boat.*

The ship headed first for Yassi Ada. Investigating wrecks there would not only help complete the survey started by Throckmorton and Kapkin the previous summer, but would also serve as a test for the gear and help everyone grow accustomed to the Turkish coast. Divers recovered a few relics, mostly amphorae that would help experts date the wrecks and determine their importance.

From Yassi Ada, the *Little Vigilant* headed down the coast, following the earlier track of the *Mandalinci*. Again, the divers investigated the wrecks that had been located the previous summer, seeking more information for the experts to work with.

Finally, the ship arrived at Cape Gelidonya. It was a rocky, bleak landfall, and the cape trailed off in a series of low, uninviting islands. A thorny shrub seemed to be the only life that the islands could support.

The *Little Vigilant* came to anchor between the two outermost islands, the spot where Captain Aras said he had found the corroded bronze relics. An underwater ridge connected the two islands, and the wreck, he had said, could be found on the top of this ridge.

But it wasn't there. And the ridge proved to be extremely uneven ground, dropping abruptly in some places from forty to one hundred feet, and broken here and there with pinnacles that rose to within ten feet of the water's surface. On either side of this uneven formation, the bottom dropped away to 150 feet or more.

The divers of *Little Vigilant* spent a full day exploring the ridge, but the only hint of a shipwreck was a rock that Kapkin brought up from the base of a ninety-foot cliff. It had a green stain on it, possibly caused by contact with a bronze object. With such scant encouragement, most of the divers were in favor of pulling anchor and searching for other wrecks in more promising waters, but Kapkin and Throckmorton pleaded for another day.

So the search continued through the following morning, but again, it produced nothing. At noon it was decided to move on. Kapkin and Throckmorton asked for one last dive. They went down a half hour before *Little*

Vigilant's scheduled departure. To fill in the time, Susan Phips and John Cochran also decided to go down. Their main goal was to shoot some underwater photos, but their dive took them to a spot where they found curiously shaped lumps of what seemed to be metal, and large, flat slabs that looked like bronze. They gathered up some of the lumps and returned to the surface.

So it was that when Kapkin and Throckmorton climbed onto the ship after another fruitless dive, they found everyone gathered around Cochran's and Phips's finds. The lumps were encrusted with lime, but as it was chipped away, bronze spear points emerged.

Cochran said the finds were made at the base of a cliff in ninety feet of water, not far from the place where Kapkin had recovered the rock with the green stain. The divers went to work at once, gathering up other metal objects and prying at the slabs of bronze. In addition to bronze picks, axes, and spear points, a few pieces of rough pottery were brought up, and when the stack of bronze slabs was finally pried loose, the divers found that they had rested upon pieces of wood and a short twist of rope. The wood and the rope fibers had been preserved by copper salts released from the bronze.

Currents around the ridge made diving dangerous. Twice divers were swept a half mile from the boat and had to be rescued with the dinghy, but despite this hazard, the crew worked for two full days. At the end of their labors, the divers had a collection of sketches and photographs, and dozens of bronze artifacts, including several flat, bronze ingots, shaped like oxhides. Gültekin said ingots of this type had not been used for at least three thousand years. It meant that the wreck dated back to the bronze age, somewhere between 1200 and 1600 B.C. It was at least a thousand years older than Sestius's wine ship.

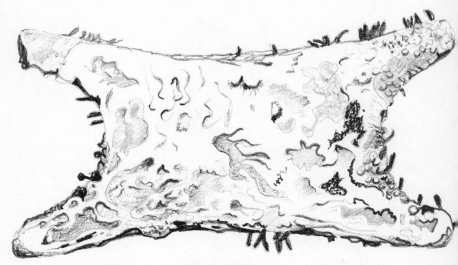

Bronze ingots in the shape of oxhides had not been used in Mediterranean trade for at least three thousand years.

With her cargo of samples from the wreck, *Little Vigilant* headed straight for Bodrum. For safekeeping, the relics were transferred to the Castle of St. Peter, a harbor fortress built by the Crusaders. The divers worked day and night to complete the cleaning, sketching, and photographing of all the finds. Then, when this work was done, Throckmorton wrote down detailed descriptions of everything and headed for the United States.

It did not take long to stimulate interest in the wreck at Cape Gelidonya. Throckmorton was soon conferring with Dr. Rodney Young, head of the Institute for Classical Archeology at the University of Pennsylvania. And Dr. Young introduced Throckmorton to George F. Bass, a graduate student at the institute specializing in the Bronze Age. The institute, Dr. Young said, would sponsor an expedition to the cape, and if Bass would learn how to dive, he could be in charge.

Things happened quickly after that. Bass crammed a ten week, YMCA diving course into six weeks. Veteran divers were recruited from five different countries. By good luck, one of those agreeing to join the expedition was Frédéric Dumas of Grand Congloué fame.

Fifteen specialists who would take part included artists, underwater photographers, surveyors, preservers of woods and metals, and of course, archeologists. It was the largest, most heavily financed, and best prepared marine archeological expedition yet organized, and as events would show, the selection of George Bass as its director woud have an impact of great benefit on expeditions in the future.

No venture in Turkish waters could be complete without Turkish sponge divers. Captain Aras with *Mandalinci* would take part and bring his friend Captain Nazif Goymen who sailed in the *Lufti Gelil,* a larger craft that would become the main workboat for the expedition.

Upon seeing the size and quality of the expedition that his reports had prompted, Throckmorton was assailed by doubts. What if it were all a mistake? What if the few pieces of bronze had simply been discarded from a passing ship and there actually was no wreck to investigate?

The doubts troubled Throckmorton right up to the day everyone arrived at Cape Gelidonya, and he still held doubts when he and Dumas made the first dive. Throckmorton led the Frenchman to an encrusted stack of ingots at the base of the ninety-foot cliff. As Throckmorton watched, Dumas inspected the area carefully. Time passed slowly, but finally the Frenchman signaled that it was time to go up. On the surface, Dumas wore a broad grin, and when he climbed out of the water he announced that the expedition appeared to be on the trail of Odysseus, one of the heroes of the Trojan War and the main hero in Homer's famous epic poem.

At the time, Dumas was speaking half in jest, but the remark proved to be prophetic.

In a more serious mood, Dumas said that a great deal of work needed to be done before anyone could guess exactly what lay below. Tons of sand must be moved and huge rocks would have to be chipped free and cleared. Precise mapping of the wreckage would be extremely difficult.

Unlike most of the wrecks that Throckmorton and Kapkin had investigated and charted, wrecks that settled gently on a smooth bottom of sand or mud, the wreck at Cape Gelidonya had fallen on a jagged, uneven ridge. As the hull rotted and broke up, the cargo had scattered in the current, leaving a trail of relics that would be hard to chart, let alone find.

The difficulties, however, did not lessen anyone's enthusiasm. Members of the expedition eagerly tackled the first job, setting up a base on shore with living quarters, a photographic darkroom, and work areas for the experts. The site chosen was at the base of a hillside spring, where fresh water could easily be impounded. The water was vital for cleaning and treating artifacts, and developing photographs.

With work at the shore station well underway, divers set a heavy anchor at the wreck site and moored it to a buoy with a stout life line. The line would serve as a hand hold against the strong currents.

At first, the Turkish divers insisted on using their conventional suits and helmets, but then Arslan was caught in the current and had to be pulled back to the *Lufti Gelil* like a fish on a line. After that the Turks learned how to use the skindiving gear, and Captain Aras no longer referred to the tanks, masks, and neoprene suits as playthings for tourists.

Before anything below was touched, surveyors, artists, and photographers swarmed over the site. Then after sea growth was cleared, more photos were taken and more sketches were made. Finally, after all loose items had been

located on the wreck map, they were gathered up in baskets and raised to the surface. Transported at once to the
shore station, the relics received the attention of the preservation experts.

With the loose relics cleared from the sea floor,
Dumas was able to start chipping on a rock overhang near
the site. It was an unnatural looking formation that had

*The hammer and chisel was soon replaced by a hydraulic jack
which saved much time and effort in freeing encrusted metal.*

sparked his curiosity during his first dive. A few minutes' work with hammer and chisel revealed that the formation was not rock at all. Instead it was an encrusted bar of bronze, welded by age to a mass of similar bars. Near this discovery, another mass that had been mistaken for rock, proved to be a heap of bronze scrap. More than a ton of bronze lay stuck to the rocky ledge or half buried in sand.

It would have taken months to chip the metal free, but Dumas speeded the work by using a hydraulic auto jack to break the seal between bronze and rock. After the *Lufti Gelil* winched the metal up to her deck in lumps, it was relatively easy to separate the individual bars and ingots.

When the last of the metal had been removed, divers found what appeared to be a small section of ship's siding. Bass dove at once and saw that small fragments of wood long buried beneath the metal had indeed survived the ages, but it was impossible from these few scraps to determine what design or construction method was followed in building the ship. Just the same, the find gave hope that other, larger sections of the hull might be discovered.

Meanwhile, the metal relics being amassed at the shore station prompted growing puzzlement and speculation. The finished spearheads, axes, and knives clearly seemed destined to supply an army, but what about the rods, ingots, and pieces of broken scrap? How could raw metal help an army already at war? And the ship evidently was to call at peaceful ports as well because the collection of finished products included plowshares, shovels, picks, hoes, needles, and cooking skewers.

The experts, sheltered in their canvas tents, worked by kerosene lamps far into the night, trying to solve the riddle. The most logical assumption seemed to be that the master of the ship was both a seaman and a smithy. As he plied his routes, he forged tools to meet the needs of trade at his next port of call. For a time, however, this remained a highly speculative theory.

The experts were more certain about the source of the raw metal. In addition to the oxhide-shaped ingots, the divers brought up pure copper molded in disks, a form that was used on Cyprus, where mines had been in operation for almost two thousand years before the birth of Christ. Further confirmation that the ship's major cargo came from Cyprus was found on some of the finished tools. They had been stamped with letters of the Cyprus-Minoan style. As yet undeciphered, this form of writing was known to be in use on Cyprus around 1200 B.C.

As for the scrap metal, it was impossible to say where it had been collected. Perhaps a little had been collected at each port of call. From the position of the metal and a few pieces of willow recovered with it, it appeared that the scrap had been carefully packed in willow baskets. This was another clue that supported the theory that the ship's owner was both a seaman and a smithy. Further support, almost conclusive, came with the discovery of an array of metal working tools—a stone anvil weighing a hundred and seventy-five pounds, a bronze forging block, several hammers, and whetstones for putting an edge on tools and weapons—all the tools needed to complete a blacksmith's shop.

But where was the ship headed? And what was its home port? These were the next questions that the archeologists tried to answer. It remained more than a romantic notion that the ship may have been headed for Troy to supply the Greeks, or the Trojans, or perhaps both with new weapons. The Plains of Troy, after all, lay two to three days sail up the Turkish coast from Cape Gelidonya. But it also seemed clear that the ship's smithy-master was a wanderer with several ports of call on his intended route. He probably changed his plans readily to take advantage of trade opportunities in metal that other mariners reported along the route.

So archeologists, never expecting to determine exactly where the ship was headed, looked for clues that would reveal its home port. Such clues, however, were elusive, and by midsummer work on the wreck was interrupted with difficulties. The air compressor used to fill the divers' tanks burned out, and diving had to stop until the machine could be repaired. Then, after an overhaul of *Mandalinci*'s motor, someone forgot to replace its oil. The ship had to sail into port for expensive repairs. This was followed by a near disaster when currents swept a diver into deep water. After a struggle, he returned to the dive boat safely, but the man lost his valuable camera.

These setbacks, combined with intense heat and swarms of stinging flies, led to discouragement. There was even some talk of abandoning the project, but then a diver surfaced one afternoon with an exciting find. It was a black stone, about an inch long and no thicker than a pencil. One surface bore a carved design. Bass gave a happy shout the moment he saw the relic.

He recognized it at once as a seal to stamp an impression into clay tablets when the clay was still wet. Used in this way, seals served as signatures that could not easily be counterfeited. This seal, showing two worshippers kneeling before a goddess, had been made in Syria some five hundred years before the shipwreck. Bass and fellow archeologists concluded that it was carried on the ship as a treasured charm, perhaps a family keepsake.

The find swept away the mood of discouragement, and divers eagerly began excavating a sand-filled pocket where the seal had been found. New discoveries came rapidly. There was an oil lamp, three balance arms for weighing metal, a plaque with a scarab design, and scarabs carved from semiprecious stones. Were these the treasures of the captain's cabin? It seemed so.

Scarabs were worshipped in many ancient cultures as sacred symbols both of fertility and life after death. Egyptian graves were often decorated with the scarab motif, but close examination of these scarabs revealed that they were not Egyptian but rather Syrian-Palestinian copies of Egyptian designs. The scarabs combined with the seal, strongly suggested a Syrian-Palestinian or Phoenician origin for the ship.

One day Throckmorton came up from the pocket that was now called the captain's cabin and climbed aboard with a smile. Extending a closed fist, he asked Bass to guess what the captain's last meal had been. The archeologist had no idea until Throckmorton opened his hand to reveal fowl and fish bones and a few olive pits, the remains of a meal eaten thirty-two hundred years ago.

Everyone on the expedition now thought of the ancient captain as a very human acquaintance, and as they learned more about him, he grew in their affection. But the nature of his ship remained a mystery.

Then, when most divers had given up hope of finding any more remains of the hull, the air pump uncovered a large rock. It was green with the stain of copper, indicating that it had been in close contact with the cargo. It took hours of work with hammer and chisel, but the rock was finally freed from surrounding formations and rolled aside. Beneath was a thin layer of sand, and below the sand, ballast stones and a section of ship siding a yard square. There was also a mass of broken sticks and twigs that puzzled the divers.

As usual, the find was plotted, sketched, and photographed before any object was moved. Then each stone, each stick, and the siding was raised to the surface.

Now the experts had solid evidence for estimating the ship's design and construction. The position and the weight of the ballast stones, combined with the weight of the metal that had been recovered led to the conclusion that the ship was about twenty-seven feet long with a beam of about six feet. Examination of the siding showed that she had been built on a keel with frames inserted after the siding had been formed into a shell. The planks had been fitted with dovetail joints to give watertight seams. The ship had been built by experts.

But the find that excited the archeologists as much as anything else was the mass of sticks and twigs, the re-mains of brushwood. In Homer's *Odyssey,* the poet wrote that Odysseus used brushwood in the construction of his ship, but the poet gave no explanation of how it was used or what purpose it served.

Now, however, the mystery was solved. The brush-wood, laid down as a matting inside the hull, protected the planks from the weight of the ballast and cargo and also insulated the ship from the chill of the sea.

Had Homer witnessed the construction of such ships? It seemed now that he had and this threw new light on a scholarly debate over his poetry. Because it was thought that the ships he described did not exist until about 1000 B.C., many scholars concluded that Homer's epic could not have been written until some two or more centuries after the conclusion of the Trojan war. But here, at Cape Gelidonya was a ship that sank at the time of the war, a ship that matched Homer's descriptions of ship construc-tion perfectly. Thus, it now is possible to say that the poet may have lived and written in an era that followed close after the war, much earlier than originally supposed.

Carbon 14 dating of organic material recovered from the wreck has established that the ship went down sometime between 1250 and 1150 B.C., and this confirms the age assumed by all archeologists who worked on the wreck.

The age is significant because it counters another long held theory, the notion that Mediterranean shipping at that time was dominated by Mycenean seamen from southern Greece or by Crete. But no Mycenean or Cretan artifacts were found on the ship. It clearly is of Phoenician origin, and it can be assumed that the Phoenicians began trading in the Eastern Mediterranean much earlier than supposed.

The work at Cape Gelidonya, as can be imagined, gave a tremendous boost to underwater archeology. The critics and the skeptics, faced with solid evidence that added to and revised our knowledge of the past, had to admit that underwater work could make a real contribution. And the work on the site set new standards of both method and technique for others to follow. Furthermore, Throckmorton's three summers in Turkish waters provide classic illustration for the three-step method now generally followed—search and location, identification, and full-scale excavation.

As for technique, the use of the best equipment, the best testing and preserving processes, and the best talent available has now become the basic rule for underwater archeology.

As a diving archeologist, Bass lifted underwater archeology to a new level of respectability. And for Bass, Cape Gelidonya was just the beginning. He returned to the University of Pennsylvania and completed work for his doctorate, using reports on the finds at Cape Gelidonya for his thesis. Then, he organized an expedition to Yassi Ada and excavated other wrecks, including a seventh century A.D. Byzantine ship that was carrying artifacts that were virtually unknown to specialists on that age.

In 1973, Bass founded the Institute of Nautical Archeology, now affiliated with Texas A&M University. The Institute trains scholars for future underwater work and its students and staff have conducted digs around the world, from the African coast to rivers in Maine.

Returning to Turkey again, Dr. Bass led the excavation of two ships in a natural cove known as Serce Liman. One proved to be a Greek ship of the second century B.C., and the other was an Islamic vessel of the eleventh century A.D. that carried a cargo of glass vases and cups. The Islamic ship may be the oldest modern vessel known, being built with planks that were fastened to a rigid framework of keel and ribs. Earlier vessels were all formed by placing ribs inside a previously fitted shell of planks.

In all his expeditions, Bass constantly experimented with new equipment and methods. He was the first to combine metal grids wth stereoptic photography to map a wreck. He later adopted cameras with extremely wide-angle lenses to facilitate the mapping process.

He was the first to develop the "phone booth" or underwater capsule where a diver can communicate with the surface, rest, and breathe fresh air, to help extend working time at a site. Bass took full advantage of sonar, the echo-sound device that detects submerged objects, and he was the first to use side-scanning sonar to obtain horizontal profiles of sunken ships. He even experimented with a two-seat submarine in the investigation of underwater sites.

Today, many governments, including Israel, France, Italy, and America, are conducting digs in the Mediterranean. All have adopted methods pioneered by Dr. Bass and the Institute. Meanwhile, Dr. Bass is training Turkish archeologists to carry on the work on that coast, which explains, in part, why the institute is the only organization licensed by the Turkish government to excavate relics from Turkish waters. Throckmorton, of course, must also take credit for the good relations between U.S. archeologists and the Turkish people. It was he who founded the Museum of Marine Archeology at Bodrum, which today houses priceless relics from all wrecks found along the Turkish coast.

So it is no exaggeration to say that the wreck at Cape Gelidonya and those who excavated it gave a firm foundation for the growth of underwater archeology as a productive international science.

PART II

Inland Waters

Chapter Six

~~~~~~~~~~~~~~~~~~~~~~~~~~~~~~~~~~~~~~

Wells of Sacrifice

The people answered the high priest's chant, but all eyes stared at the girl. Blue dye covered her young body. A crown of white feathers enclosed her black hair, and gold glittered at her throat and wrists. She stood proudly, surrounded by the haze of smoke from burning incense. A sweet smell filled the air.

When the chanting stopped, the priest made a sign. At once, two men stepped forward, lifted the girl, and threw her over the edge of the cliff. She fell silently to splash in the dark water. The crown of feathers floated at the center of a widening ring of ripples, but the girl sank to the depths, never to be seen again.

Then, when the chanting resumed, small splashes dotted the water's surface as the people made their offerings—jewelry of gold and jade, bowls filled with cacao beans, carved figurines, and chunks of copal, the sweet-smelling incense.

This visage of Chac, easily identified by his long nose, decorates the corner of a building at Chichén Itzá.

Why was the girl killed? Why did the people throw their most valued possessions into the well?

All was done for Chac, the great Mayan god, the bringer of rain and renewed life. Chac was all-powerful, and the people believed their lives rested in his hands. They had enduring faith in him.

But there was another reason for the grim and often-repeated ritual at the sacred well, a deeper reason found in the earth itself.

Mexico's Yucatan peninsula, a land ruled by the Maya for at least a thousand years, has thin soil covering a porous layer of limestone. Water seeps quickly through the soil and into the limestone. Surface water is thus scarce and irrigation impossible. So crops can be raised only through the summer and autumn when rain falls almost daily.

This is the situation today, and it was the situation

when the Maya ruled the Yucatan and achieved their advanced level of civilization. Their religion was complex. Their temple cities were awesome, and their trade network was vast. It is often difficult to remember that this civilization was based on a very simple economy—the family garden, where beans, squash, and corn were grown. When rain failed and the corn stalks withered, the very foundations of Mayan culture shook.

The people then could look only to their priests, the men of mystery who knew how to appease Chac and bring rain. Chac could best be served by a human sacrifice, a young girl to pass into the world beyond and be the great god's bride, or a man to serve his godly needs. Of course, all valuables the people might add to the offering were bound to help—anything that would persuade Chac to stop withholding the precious rain.

Fortunately, for basic survival in the dry season—winter and spring—there were many wells, or *cenotes,* what we would call sinkholes. These occurred where the limestone had collapsed, exposing pools of water sixty to eighty feet below the ground. The level of water in these pools, supplied by seepage, was stable, so even in the driest months, the people had water for their needs. But without pumps or irrigation canals, it was not possible to use water from the *cenotes* to raise the all-important corn.

When Chac could not be persuaded by gifts or sacrifice to bring rain for the crops, the people moved into the forest to eat roots, tree bark, and leaves. The old and the sick were usually left behind to die. And normal living died, not to be revived again until the rain returned.

With this uncertain life of feast or famine, it is a wonder that the Maya were able to build an empire. In size and grandeur, many of the structures in their cities rivaled the pyramids of Egypt. In beauty, many Mayan buildings were a match for the Parthenon. Mayan scholars invented a written language and wrote books. Mayan astronomers developed an accurate calendar. Mayan mathematicians mastered the concept of zero and developed a numbering system, based on units of twenty, that allowed them to fix all the dates of their long history.

But when explorers gazed on the abandoned Mayan temples in the last century, little was known of their culture. It was thought for many years that the buildings were the work of a lost civilization, a mysterious people who left the Yucatan long before the Spanish conquest of Mexico early in the sixteenth century.

Diego de Landa, however, knew the truth. He knew that the Indians who peopled the Yucatan at the time of the conquest were, in fact, Maya, survivors of the great civilization. It was Landa's duty as first bishop of Merida, the Spanish capital of colonial Yucatan, to convert these Indians from pagan idolatry to Christianity. In his zeal, the Franciscan monk sometimes used harsh methods, and he committed the unforgivable sin of burning all the Mayan books he could find, calling them works of the devil. Today, just three of these books exist, and little of the writing they contain has been deciphered.

Yet, despite his zeal, Landa appreciated the Indians and their past. He interviewed them and wrote down all he could about their ancient customs. Then, when called back to Spain to answer charges of cruelty against the natives, charges that were eventually withdrawn, Landa published his research. Unfortunately, *Relacion de las Cosas de Yucatan* (Report on Yucatan Affairs) was intended largely as Landa's defense against the charges he faced and as such was dismissed and soon forgotten.

So when two intrepid travelers, John L. Stephens, the writer, and Frederick Catherwood, the artist, pub-

lished their report on the amazing Mayan ruins in Yucatan
and Guatemala in the 1840s, it was still believed by many
scholars that a "lost civilization" had built the structures
and then vanished from the face of the earth.

This romantic notion did not appeal to Edward
Herbert Thompson, the American consul in Merida, who
began investigating the Mayan temples in 1899. Thompson was particularly interested in the ruins of Chichén
Itzá, once the leading religious center of the Yucatan.
He managed to buy a large block of land there and begin
clearing the jungle surrounding the buildings.

Although an amateur archeologist, Thompson was a
serious scholar, and his research led him to Landa's Spanish text. Thompson did not exactly rediscover the book,
but he was one of the first of his day to take it as a factual
account of the Maya and their customs. And there was
one passage about a sacred *cenote* at Chichén Itzá that
riveted Landa's attention.

"In times of drought," Landa reported, "the Mayans
threw living human beings into this well. . . . They also
threw many other things such as jewels."

Jewels, perhaps gold and other valuables, presented
an undeniable attraction to all archeologists of Thompson's day. Treasure stimulated keen interest in the young
science of digging into the past. But Thompson also knew
that finding treasure in the well at Chichén Itzá would
confirm his faith in Bishop Landa as an authentic chron-
icler of the Mayan culture.

Chichén Itzá lies in the heart of the Yucatan peninsula. It contains the ruins of two distinct cultures, early
Mayan and late Mayan, which was influenced by Toltec
invaders from Central Mexico. As a land archeologist,
Thompson thus had much to occupy his time and interests, but he walked again and again to the edge of the

sacred well. The sinkhole had a diameter of 180 feet and the water lay eighty feet below its rim. A few building stones at one spot near the rim suggested that a small temple once stood there, and perhaps it was from this temple that the victims were hurled into the well.

But were there really human sacrifices here or was the tale nothing more than Landa's justification in his treatment of the Maya? The only way to answer the question was to excavate the well, and at the time, Thompson lacked both the equipment and the funds to do the job.

After ten years spent on the land excavations at Chichén Itzá, however, Thompson returned to the United States and conferred with representatives of the Peabody Foundation at Harvard University, which had helped finance his work. He persuaded them to back an excavation of the sacred well.

To prepare for the work, Thompson learned how to use the heavy helmet and suit, the only diving gear available at that time. The main equipment for the dig, however, was to be a suction dredge.

Work began in 1909. Thompson soon discovered that the water in the well was too murky and visibility too limited for productive diving. So the dredge was put to work, but it, too, seemed to be less than satisfactory.

Days and days went by with Thompson stationed at the dredge outlet, screening and examining the black mud that gushed up from the bottom. The mud reeked with the decay of leaves and branches that had fallen into the well. A discouraged Thompson wondered if the only reward for his efforts was to be a bad smell. But finally, the dredge brought up two lumps of copal, the treasured incense that the Maya got from the sap of a tree. It was tested in fire, and Thompson and his native workers whiffed a new smell—success.

More finds followed. Tools, weapons, fragments of clay bowls, pieces of cloth, and jewelry of jade and gold came up through the dredge. Thompson tried diving again. Working almost entirely by touch, he found more jewelry, carved figurines, and human bones, which proved to be remains of females. He continued diving and recovered ceramic incense burners, axes, lance and arrow points, copper chisels, disks of beaten copper, clay vases and plates, more human bones, and many more chunks of copal.

The relics that Thompson brought up from the sacred well can be seen today in the Anthropological Museum in Mexico City. They are valued at two million dollars, but the worth to archeology is beyond measure because their discovery proved that Bishop Landa's account of Mayan culture was valid. Today, thanks to Thompson's work at Chichén Itzá, Landa's book is the foundation for all studies of the Maya.

Of course, by today's standards, Thompson's methods were crude. The suction dredge broke many fragile relics, and even though he dove to recover many objects, he did not record the position of the things he found. And unfortunately, when Thompson finished his work at the well, scholars generally concluded that he had cleaned it out, that nothing more remained to be discovered. This of course, discouraged further excavation, and after a 1925 Mexican expedition to Chichén Itzá found nothing in the well, interest evaporated.

When a team of divers next recovered relics in the Yucatan it was from a different well. This well, or *cenote,* was located several miles east of Chichén Itzá in the ruins of a large Mayan city known as Dzibilchaltun (Dzeeb-eel-chal-toon) , a Mayan word which means "where there is writing on flat stone." Here the remains of many stone

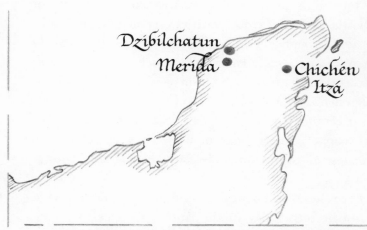

Merida, established by the Spanish, is the modern capital, while Dzibilchaltun and Chichén Itzá, built by the Maya, are ancient capitals of Yucatan.

buildings sprawl between the modern city of Merida and the north coast of Yucatan.

There are several unusual things about Dzibilchaltun. For one thing, it appears to be very old, dating back many centuries before the birth of Christ. Most Mayan cities were not established until after the birth of Christ. Also, Dzibilchaltun had a large population, estimated, from house platforms that have been discovered, to have numbered in the thousands. Other Mayan cities were inhabited only by priests and rulers. People from the surrounding farmland went to these cities to worship, but they did not live there permanently.

Excavation of Dzibilchaltun began in 1956, under the direction of E. W. Andrews of Tulane University. In his first season, his crews concentrated on land excavation, but a large *cenote* intrigued Andrews. He did not know if it simply supplied water for the ancient city or if it served as a sacred well.

Fortunately, two vacationing students, David Conkle and Whitney Robbinet from the University of Florida, both skin divers, visited the site. They were traveling with their diving gear, and it took very little persuasion by Andrews to arrange an exploratory dive.

Success was immediate. Conkle and Robbinet discovered what seemed to be an endless supply of relics— pieces of worked flint, earplugs of carved bone, many pottery fragments, and rarest of all, unbroken pots. Land excavators had little chance of finding unbroken pots in picked over ruins, but the water of the well had preserved these pots and hidden them from thieves and vandals. Andrews was particularly excited about the finds because they seemed to date from a very early stage of Mayan culture.

Conkle and Robbinet reported that the well slanted so that one side formed an overhanging roof while the other made a steeply slanting floor. The visiting divers never reached the bottom of the well, but they recovered an impressive collection of relics, including almost three thousand fragments of pottery. Much work, however, remained to be done.

When Andrews returned in 1957 with a larger expedition backed by the National Science Foundation, the American Philosophical Society, and the National Geographic Society, he was prepared for a full exploration of the *cenote*.

The diving team consisted of Fernando Euan and Earl Brecht of Mexico, and Bates Littlehales and Luis Marden of the United States. Littlehales and Marden, both photographers for the *National Geographic,* were eager to put their underwater cameras to work. They dove first, intending to explore the full dimensions of the well.

Lily pads on the surface gave the water below a dark

Shadow from the overhanging wall of limestone turns the deep waters of the cenote *inky black.*

green hue, but this light quickly gave way to shadow as the divers descended. They had to turn on their flashlights to inspect the sloping wall of the well. At the eighty-foot level they came upon a break in the slope, a muddy shelf where an old tree trunk and two stones had lodged. One stone was rectangular and the other was round, possibly a section of a building column. Below the shelf, the wellside fell away abruptly.

The diver's lights seemed like feeble cones in the gloom, but they continued their descent until the well finally leveled off in a muddy bottom. There they discovered a tunnel. Marden edged inside. Littlehales, who followed, spotted the broken neck of a large jar and pulled it from the mud. A cloud of oily silt rose with the jar, blacking out all visibility. For several seconds their lights were useless. The divers almost panicked, but by putting their hands on the top of the tunnel, they were able to orient themselves and work their way out.

Back on the surface, Littlehales handed up the jar fragment that had caused the trouble. It was the first relic of the season to be brought up from the well.

Thousands more followed. After setting an anchor and safety line and after building a diving platform and a hoisting derrick, the four divers went to work filling collection baskets, first from the sixty-foot level and then from eighty feet down. Pottery fragments dominated the early finds, but there were also many worked stones that had fallen into the well. These appeared to have come from a building that had once stood near the rim.

Here was an obvious parallel with the *cenote* at Chichén Itzá, which also once had a structure at its edge, but Andrews was not convinced that the Dzibilchaltun well had been used in the same manner. He thought at first that the well was simply a source of water for the city, and the relics being recovered were the remains of jugs and other things that had been dropped accidentally.

When Littlehales and Euan each found long pins carved from bone and decorated with Mayan writing, Andrews did not change his view. The pins, probably used to hold women's hair, could easily have been lost when water jugs were being filled.

The divers next brought up a clay flute, a small head carved from stone, bone noseplugs, and several pieces of obsidian. Had these been offered to the rain god? Andrews could not say.

Even when the divers began bringing up human bones, Andrews remained cautious about drawing any conclusions. The bones, he said, might simply be evidence of accidental drownings. Divers, after all, were also bringing up the bones of cows and rodents that had fallen into the well and drowned.

But more human bones appeared. Some skulls were flattened on the top, supporting Landa's description of the Mayan practice of tying pieces of wood to the heads of infants to force elongation of their skulls. The bone collection included the remains of both men and women, some still in their youth at the time of death. An unusually large thighbone presented a puzzle. Could it have been the remains of a Spaniard from the time of conquest who was captured by Mayan warriors and sacrificed in the well? It was possible.

Beneath the tree stump at the eighty-foot level, the divers found several large jugs, some in perfect condition,

A large, unbroken bowl and a human skull helped confirm suspicions that the well at Dzibilchaltun was sacred to the Maya.

and nearby, Marden found a sea fan, a beautiful coral formation that could only have come from the ocean. A ritual offering? Maybe.

Marden's wife, Ethel, and Dr. Charles Aquardo, a Navy diving specialist, joined the crew at Dzibilchaltun, and Ethel Marden soon made a significant discovery, a clay jaguar, about eight inches high, the first figurine brought up from the well. Later, other divers found a jade bead, a finger ring carved from bone, a cylinder of crystal, and a small, open-mouthed mask carved from wood with a double topknot hairdress. It was soon discovered that the crystal cylinder fit perfectly in the mouth of the mask.

Even Andrews had to admit that these relics were not likely to have been casually lost. They must have been thrown in the well on purpose. He concluded that during at least some periods of the history of Dzibilchaltun, the well was used for ritual, which very likely included human sacrifices.

Marden and Littlehales themselves one day very nearly became victims of the well after they explored the deep tunnel. They went fifty feet into it, and reached a depth of 144 feet below the surface without finding any end to the tunnel. Although they then followed an ascent schedule of twenty-five feet per minute, Marden's right arm began to hurt soon after he surfaced. He put on a fresh air tank and dove at once to eighty feet. The pain went away, but it returned when he came up again. Fellow divers next rushed him to Merida and put him in a make-shift decompression tank. The tank could not handle the necessary pressure, however, and then Littlehales developed spinal pain that was so severe he could not sit down.

Fortunately, the U.S. Navy was able to respond

quickly to a call for help. A four-motor Navy plane sped to Merida, picked up the two divers and flew them to the Navy's Mine Defense Laboratory in Panama City, Florida. After forty-four hours in the decompression chamber there, Marden and Littlehales emerged cured of the bends.

They returned to Yucatan and resumed diving, but the work at the well was all but finished. They had helped prove that there was more than one sacred well in the Mayan empire.

Meanwhile, at Chichén Itzá, preparations were afoot for another exploration of the *cenote* there. Members of the Frogman Club of Mexico became interested in the *cenote* after some exploratory dives in 1954, and this interest eventually led to the organization of a joint United States–Mexican expedition that was financed largely by the National Geographic Society. Members of the expedition believed that many artifacts had been missed by Thompson because he had dredged a top soft layer of mud only. An uderlying layer of harder mud was still to be excavated, and an air lift seemed to be just the tool for the job. Work began in the fall of 1960.

Visibility in the murky water was limited to about two inches, but working by feel, the divers mapped the bottom of the well before installing the air lift. It was suspended from a barge that also served as the diving platform.

When the motor of the air compressor roared to life, muddy water immediately began gushing from the lift and splashing on the catch screen. Within minutes, the man tending the screen gave a shout and held up a ball of copal. Soon other balls of the incense rolled onto the screen.

Meanwhile divers began bringing up relics. One man

Chichén Itzá's well began yielding more relics when an air lift, mounted on a barge, went to work in 1960.

came up with an unbroken clay bowl, and another surfaced with a foot-high figurine fashioned from native rubber.

Stones that had fallen from the temple presented a hazard because they were easily dislodged and could roll down on an unwary diver. Fortunately there were no serious injuries. The dirty water of the *cenote* was another problem. It caused eye and ear infections and upset stomachs, all of which forced loss of diving time. Just the same the expedition was a success, proving beyond doubt that Thompson had dredged up just a small fraction of the well's treasures.

In all, the expedition recovered more than four thousand artifacts, including pieces of jade, sea coral, and amber, arrowheads of obsidian and flint, clay pots and dishes, idols made of wood, clay, and jade, many balls of copal, and human skulls. There were also treasures of gold —earplugs, arm loops, rings, rattles, bells, cups, engraved disks, sandals, and a breastpiece shaped like a turtle shell and hung with three rattles.

There seemed to be an endless supply of treasure, but after four months, the work was abruptly halted by Dr. Eusebio Davalos Hurtado, director of the Institute of Anthropology and History in Mexico City where the relics were being examined. He said that the air lift had damaged some of the fragile objects and that the position of items was not being recorded accurately enough to get a clear picture of their stratigraphic location in the well bottom. This made it impossible to date the finds because recent relics from the top of the mud were being mixed up with older relics brought up from lower levels.

Norman Scott, one of the United States members of the expedition and an expert on the use of the air lift, realized that other methods would have to be used to satisfy the director's requirements. Scott worked up two plans. The first was to try to drain the *cenote* and turn it into a dry-land dig. If this did not work, he suggested an alternate approach, using chemicals to clear the water so that archeologists could work with the divers and supervise the recovery of relics. Dr. Hurtado approved both plans, but it took time to raise the necessary funds for the undertaking.

Work did not resume until the fall of 1967. The new expedition arrived with more than a hundred workers and massive equipment including a derrick with twenty-five-ton lifting strength, a one thousand-square-foot raft, two huge pumps, and heavy suction hoses. The derrick first lowered the raft to the water. The biggest pump and suction hoses followed. Another pump remained at the rim of the well to serve as a booster for the draining operation.

Scott estimated that it would take twenty-three days to empty the well provided that more water did not seep into it from the surrounding limestone formation.

Pumping began on September 23. The water level dropped a foot the first day, and seven feet after six days. This was enough to expose a mudbank around the rim of the bottom and allow archeologists to begin dry-land excavation. It soon became obvious, however, that water was seeping in almost as fast as it was being pumped out and the pumps never would empty the well completely. Some work would have to be done by divers.

Scott decided to try to clean the water and improve visibility with chlorine. The attempt almost ended in tragedy when a tank of the deadly gas leaked, poisoning the air in the well. Fortunately, the derrick operator was able to lift the nineteen workers in the well to safety before anyone was seriously harmed.

As an alternate project, a filtering system was devised. The well water was run through the filter and treated with chemicals that removed suspended particles. In four days, underwater visibility was increased from just a few inches to eight feet. Some divers began removing rocks and debris from the well bottom while others gave diving lessons to archeologists on the site, preparing them for recovery of relics. Five more days of filtering increased visibility to thirty feet, making it possible to photograph relics on the bottom before they were lifted to the surface. With such good visibility, it was now safe to use the air lift to clear mud. Conditions were so good, in fact, that the entire operation could now be handled as an underwater excavation. The pumps were closed down, and as the water rose to its normal level, the dry-land work was abandoned.

The excavation of the *cenote* at Chichén Itzá continued until April, 1968, when the last of the expedition's funds were expended. Scott estimated that just three months more work would have completed the job, but neither he nor any others on the crew were disappointed with their achievements.

More than six thousand artifacts had been recovered. They included two wooden stools, the first pieces of Mayan furniture ever discovered. Snake heads carved on the stools had open mouths and in each mouth the head of a man was depicted. Other items, including dolls made of rubber, wax, and wood, pieces of cloth, carved staghorn and bone, many beads, and relics made of copper and jade, stone knives, projectile points, and a big collection of incense, gave new insights on Mayan life.

The gold relics alone showed highly refined skill and artistry. One of the finest relics was a pair of child's sandals made of hammered gold leaf.

From the numerous skulls and other human bones collected, archeologists have estimated that four to five hundred souls were sacrificed in the sacred well. The Maya, obviously, had an enduring faith in the great god Chac, the bringer of rain and renewer of life.

Chapter Seven

~~~~~~~~~~~~~~~~~~

The Lake People

Lakes are a very rich source of archeological information, and because fresh water has fewer corrosive chemicals and usually supports less sea growth than salt water, the relics recovered from lakes are often remarkably well preserved.

Many fine figurines, incense burners, and other objects recovered from lakes in Mexico and Guatemala suggest that the custom of throwing valuables into water as a religious ritual had early origins predating the Mayan tradition by many centuries.

The salvage of the remains of two, flat-bottomed boats from the shallow waters of New York's Lake George have given scholars the only samples of utility boats, known as bateaux, which were in wide use during early American colonial times. Until these hulks were raised, scholars had nothing more than two drawings that gave an imperfect idea of the nature of this type of boat.

Efforts to salvage two luxury ships that sank in Lake Nemi near Rome in the first century A.D. began in 1446 and continued off and on without success until our own century when the Italian dictator Mussolini ordered the lake partially drained to allow dry-land salvage. Unfortunately, the two large ships with ornate carvings and tile-covered decks were destroyed by fire near the close of World War II, but they were available for inspection long enough for scholars to learn what kind of vessel Roman emperors used for their pleasure cruising.

But lakes of the European Alps lead all other inland waters in archeological interest. Alpine lake excavations date back to the unusually dry winter of 1853–54 when there was an extreme drop in water levels.

In Switzerland, the lake levels dropped so low that many of the people living along their shores decided to add the exposed land to their property by building coffer dams around it. The work led to discovery, and early in 1854, Ferdinand Keller, head of Zurich's Antiquarian Society, received a visitor, a lakeside dweller who carried a bundle of Stone Age implements.

Eagerly Keller examined the axes, flaked knives, and scrapers that the man spread before him. Did these crude tools have a connection with the submerged pole fields? The fields, covered with the stumps of many vertical poles, had already been found in Alpine lakes of Germany, Austria, Italy, and France as well as in Switzerland. So far, however, no one had been able to explain them.

Keller began an intensive investigation of the pole fields in Lake Zurich. The low water level made it easy to locate the fields and inspect the bottom. In many cases it was possible to see artifacts lying in plain view beneath the shallow water.

Using scrapers and long-handled tongs, Keller brought up an extensive collection of stone tools. Then he published reports of his discoveries, which sparked wide interest. Before long, relic hunters were tonging up artifacts from lakes throughout the Alps. Even after wet winters returned and the lakes rose to their normal levels, the search continued. Fishermen found that they could earn a better livelihood by selling relics than by selling fish.

Tools of the Bronze Age as well as the Stone Age were brought up and sold by the thousands with little attempt to identify, sort, or catalogue the finds. Such activity added almost nothing to knowledge of the ancient people who populated the region. And for years it was erroneously assumed that the finds marked a culture of lake dwellers who built their homes on stilts above the water.

Though crudely formed, Stone Age pottery recovered from Lake Zurich shows variety in both shape and decoration.

Such construction would require more technical skill and more sophisticated equipment than the ancients possessed, but the idea persisted. After all, stilt homes located away from shore could be easily defended, and they would be ideal for communities of fishermen. Keller himself endorsed the stilt house idea, and those who followed him did not question it.

Friedrich Schwab, a colonel in the Swiss army, made the next big contribution to the study of lake people. Soon after Keller's reports appeared, Schwab began searching for pole fields in the Lake of Neuchâtel west of Lake Zurich. He probed the bottom with a special pair of tongs that he had designed for the search. It was close to shore in three feet of water at the base of an old wall near the town of La Tène that he made his most amazing discovery —a vast collection of bronze spearheads and swords.

The craftsmanship and design of the weapons showed they had been made by Celts, who dominated the area from 400 B.C. to at least 50 A.D. Identified today as La Tène Culture, its people followed trade routes that reached into southern Russia and perhaps all the way to the Orient. Schwab had a glass window fitted into the bottom of his rowboat and spent three years bringing up artifacts from the site. In addition to weapons he found fine pottery and jewelry made of enamel, coral, bronze, and gold. In 1862, the site was diked and pumped dry so that excavation could continue as a land dig. La Tène and other sites related to it have brought new respect for the advanced craftsmanship of people of prehistoric Europe.

Later, finds in other lakes gave evidence of an earlier Bronze Age culture that flourished between 1200 and 800 B.C. Again, it was assumed that these people also built their houses on stilts over the water. No one could guess what the ancient houses looked like until remains of a village were unearthed, not in a lake but in a boggy, Alpine field where workers were cutting peat for fuel. Floors and parts of the thatched roofs as well as the vertical poles were unearthed.

Professor Hans Reinerth, who investigated the site, gathered so many details on house construction that it was possible to recreate two prehistoric villages on the shores

Lake Constance models follow the ancient design in all but one detail. They stand on stilts over the water.

of Lake Constance. The houses, with sides of vertical poles and woven reeds and roofs of thick thatch, are said to be faithful copies of the original structures. But there is one thing wrong. They stand over the water.

Professor Reinerth himself was beginning to suspect that Keller's stilt dwelling theory was wrong. Peat field samples, after all, had been found on land. Perhaps the drowned pole fields had also once been on land.

But it was not until 1940 that Oskar Paret, a German

engineer and prehistory researcher who had spent years studying Alpine finds, stated firmly that the villages could not have been built over the water. His conclusion was based in part on the simple fact that modern derricks and pile drivers had been needed to build the model villages. It was also found that recently built stilt houses on Lake Atter in Austria had fallen into the water in just a few years. Their poles had rotted away at the water line. Only poles impregnated with modern chemicals didn't rot.

Paret's conclusion was that the prehistoric houses had been built on the shores of the Alpine lakes at a time when they had been reduced by dry climate to small bodies of water. When wet climate returned, with the snow and rainfall typical of today's Alpine weather, the lake levels rose, drowning the shoreline settlements.

Today, although an image of stilt houses still remains in the public mind, scholars generally agree with Paret's conclusions. The flooding of the ruins was fortunate because lake water has preserved countless relics that would have been broken by plows, scattered, sold into private collections, or simply lost had they remained exposed on land. And despite early work, the full value of the lake sites could not be fully realized until the development of the Aqualung and scientific techniques for excavating underwater. While it was true that many of the early researchers were careful and conscientious men, working from the surface with tongs or rakes had severe limitations. A stone axe by itself might tell a good deal about the stone worker's skill and cultural development, but it told little about the people who used it.

To gain all possible knowledge from a find it had to be examined in its original position so that its level as compared with surrounding relics could be noted and the surrounding soil examined.

The Aqualung opened the way for such precise examination, but special techniques were also needed. Visibility in the windswept lakes was usually very poor, particularly in shallow water where wind kept water in a constant agitation that stirred up silt. Also most of the lakes supported a heavy growth of plankton, which further clouded the water. Little work could be accomplished waiting for a calm day when the water was relatively clear. So it was often necessary to work by feel alone.

The French archeologist Raymond Laurent solved many of the problems in his pioneer work that began on French lakes in 1952. He found that the conventional square grid that had been successful in charting the position of finds in the Mediterranean was almost useless in cloudy water. To measure the position of an object in relation to the square grid, it was necessary to take a right-angle fix on two sides of the square and then measure the distance from the fix point to the nearest corner. It was easy to make errors with this system, so Laurent developed a framework of equal-sided triangles that could be lowered over a site. To record the position of a relic with a triangle it was only necessary to take the distance from two angles of the triangle. By preattaching measuring tape to all angles of the frame, it was simple for a diver to take error-free measurements.

Laurent's greatest contribution to lake archeology, however, was a new standard of thoroughness. Every man-made object, he said, must be plotted and brought up for study. Laurent also introduced excavation of lake bottoms, recovering objects that had been buried beneath mud and silt as well as those that lay on the bottom's surface, and he was careful to preserve the stratigraphic record in lake bottom excavations so that the age sequence of finds could be maintained. Many of the latest dry land techniques such as frequent soil sampling and pollen counts were also adopted by Laurent.

His thorough methods were adopted by other lake archeologists. The result was that excavations now yielded far more information with far greater detail than ever before. By the mid-1960s Ulrich Rouff had introduced the Laurent system to work in Switzerland's Lake Zurich, and Rouff added a new invention to the underwater archeologist kit of tools—the water curtain.

It was a simple device, simply a water pipe punctured with a row of small holes. The pipe, linked by hose to a water pump, was lowered into position at one side of a work area. Then clear water was pumped into the pipe to produce a wide flow from the row of small holes. The flow drove clouded water away from the dig.

In the early 1970s, five French archeologist-divers agreed that the Laurent system could be further refined by recovering all objects whether man-made or not. Aimé Bocquet, Francoise Ballet, Patrick Grandjean, Christian Orcel, and Alain Cura decided to apply this technique to a Stone Age site off the southern shore of Lake Paladru in eastern France.

Enlisted to work with the divers was a crew of specialists who would sift the soil for tiny relics, bones, wood chips, bark, leaves, fragments of nutshell, and pollen. An area totalling fifteen hundred square meters was marked off for excavation. Considering the difficulties ahead of them, the divers had launched an ambitious undertaking.

The water, even in summer, was cold, and to avoid painful numbness and impairment of judgment from thickened blood, the divers were forced to surface and rest frequently. Although a water curtain helped, visibility was so restricted that the divers usually had to work by touch only. Also, the bottom strata was overlaid by a thick coating of mud that rose in inky clouds whenever it was disturbed.

Because the mud was a recent accumulation containing no ancient relics or evidence, the divers decided to remove it with a suction dredge. The dredging laid bare a crumbly formation of thin, lake-bottom strata.

All digging in these strata was done by hand to make sure that nothing would be missed. If a diver could feel no objects in a secton of strata, it was scraped carefully into a bucket and carried ashore where the soil could be sifted and analyzed by the specialists. When contact was made with an object, the diver cleared the soil around it, plotted its position and, if visibility permitted, took a picture of it before taking it to the surface.

If the strata was too crumbly for this method of search, chunks of soil were lifted in blocks to be dismantled and studied in detail on shore. Lifting soil in blocks proved to be the only practical way to preserve fragile relics such as woven fabric or baskets.

Workers on shore had a hard time keeping up with the divers. All objects had to be weighed, numbered, and recorded. Organic material such as wood or seeds had to be sealed in plastic to prevent drying. Pottery fragments had to be cleaned and treated with liquid plastic.

Special attention was given to the house posts that had been preserved in the soil. By counting and measuring the growth rings in these posts and comparing the rings with other ancient remains of wood in the area, experts were not only able to estimate the age of the posts but also to say in what season of the year the trees were felled to make them.

In all, 810 house posts were recovered, and they, combined with Carbon 14 dating of other organic remains, established that the little settlement had flourished on the shores of Lake Paladru five thousand years ago. After seven years of painstaking work, the French archeologists can tell us in amazing detail how these Stone Age people lived.

When first occupied, the settlement stood on a grassy headland that jutted into a lake that was a good deal smaller than it is today. The site was occupied twice, the first settlers apparently arriving from a nearby village in about 2900 B.C. The people were farmers and were probably attracted by good grazing land in the meadows around the shore of the lake. There were also thick stands of fir trees nearby that provided ready building material.

Trees for the houses were felled in the winter. The branches were trimmed and the logs were stacked, but construction was not begun until the following winter after more trees were cut. The first house was a rectangular structure, four meters wide and twelve meters long. A single door in one of the long walls faced north. A fire hearth was located in the center of the building.

The house was framed on vertical posts supporting horizontal beams that in turn supported a gabled roof, probably thatched with lake reeds. The framework was lashed together with vines, and the space between the poles was filled with smaller poles set vertically in a trench to form the walls of the house.

At first, the only other structure in the settlement was a fence across the neck of the headland. The fence and the lakeshore made an enclosure to hold farm animals.

A year after the first house went up, another almost exactly like it was built to the south. It ran parallel to and just 1.2 meters away from the first. And again, the single door faced north. This settlement was occupied for thirty years.

The people gathered shellfish from the shore of the

Two dwellings and a livestock fence were the main structures in the Stone Age settlement on the shore of Lake Paladru.

lake and fished with nets, probably from dugout canoes. Wheat, flax and other crops were cultivated apparently after trees and underbrush had been cleared with fire. Hunters brought home bear, deer, birds, and rabbits. The domestic animals included pigs, beef cattle, goats, and sheep. They provided wool and leather as well as milk and meat.

The people added variety to their diet by gathering acorns, hazelnuts, beachnuts, blackberries, wild apples, and wild plums. Apparently some nut trees were cultivated because the nuts were larger than the average wild samples found in the area.

Crudely fired pots and woven baskets served for food storage. Clothing was woven from flax and wool, and a collection of thread balls, loom combs, and spindles found at the site suggested that all was woven at home. No cloth was imported.

Wheat, milled into coarse flour on granite stones, was baked in flat loaves. The clay hearth did duty for both roasting of meat and baking. Pot cooking was done by heating quartzite pebbles and dropping them into the cooking pot to bring it to a boil.

The people showed just fair stone-working skill. Most tools were roughly shaped by striking flakes from the local flint, but occasionally the more precise pressure flaking technique was used with flakes removed by pressing rather than striking the stone.

Though indifferent stone workers, the people excelled in shaping wood. Wooden spoons recovered from the site would be a match for wooden spoons found in the modern kitchen. Handles for stone tools were fashioned with care. One stone axe had a handle with a hand grip made of antler. The antler, in the shape of a sleeve, fitted over the wooden shaft to cushion the hands against the vibration of chopping blows. Two flint knives were recovered with wooden handles intact, and several other tools had traces of wooden handles.

Other relics included many stone weights for fish nets and pieces of the nets themselves. A copper fish hook caused considerable surprise. Metal, according to scholars, did not come into use in the area until well after 3000 B.C. The fish hook must have been a rare and prized possession.

During the ninth year of occupation, the posts for the first house apparently rotted away forcing a complete reconstruction. And after another nine years, both houses were rebuilt, again probably because of rot. The new buildings varied little from the original structures.

The level of Lake Paladru rose and fell during the period of occupation bringing the shoreline close to the houses, but the people were not flooded out. Instead, it seems that fire destroyed the settlement, and the place was abandoned. Alders, elms, and ash trees invaded the clearing, and then it was flooded. A thin layer of silt and the residue of reeds covered the burned remains of the houses.

About sixty years after the site was abandoned, the lake level dropped to expose the headland once more. Farmers returned to establish a new settlement. The people may well have been descendants of the first settlers. Pottery and tools from the second settlement differed little from pottery and tools of the first, but there were some slight differences. Houses of the second settlement, instead of being rectangular were almost square, and the people sometimes used bark as a floor covering. The first settlers had used fern and fir boughs to cover their floors.

The archeologists cannot say exactly how long the second settlement was occupied or what caused it to be abandoned, but there were few other questions left unanswered about the Stone Age people of Lake Paladru. And the many details gathered about these people and their culture make it difficult to remember that this was an underwater excavation. No dry-land dig has been more thorough and exacting.

Chapter Eight

~~~~~~~~~~~~~~~~~~~~~~~~~~

The Ironclads

River archeology presented scientists with a new set of difficulties. Because of shifting silt and mud, a stratified river bottom is rare. Strong currents can make diving hard work at best. White water rapids are downright dangerous. Where currents are not swift, river waters are often clouded with suspended silt and mud particles. But despite the difficulties, river archeology has added greatly to our knowledge of the past.

Bronze Age swords and axes have been dredged from the Lea, Nahe, Saône, Schelt, Seine, Weser, and Thames rivers. Mastodon bones have been recovered from rivers in Florida, and some of these rivers have also yielded a collection of artifacts from early nineteenth century military posts. Such fragile relics as bottles and clay pipes, almost always found in pieces on dry land sites, have been recovered intact in the protective silt of Florida rivers.

Anchors, cannons and other eighteenth century nautical relics have been recovered from the York River where several British ships went down in an attempt to block river entry by a French fleet near the close of the American War of Independence.

Cooking pots, iron axes, spear points, musket balls, lead for molding bullets, whetstones, and flint have been recovered in very difficult dives from river rapids in Minnesota where canoes and their cargoes were lost by early fur traders. Shipping records helped date these relics, and the relics in turn helped date many Indian settlements and trading posts where similar finds were made.

But by far the most dramatic achievement in river archeology so far took place in the State of Mississippi, where a unique Civil War ship was raised from the Yazoo River. The story begins almost 120 years ago with one of the war's oddest naval engagements.

Soon after the clanking steam engine broke the morning's silence, the strange ship appeared. With twin stacks spewing smoke and Old Glory fluttering from her mast, the ironclad *Cairo* slowly negotiated one of the many sharp turns of the Yazoo River. She moved like a girl at her first dance—tentatively. But this was deceptive. The *Cairo* was the most feared ship in the Union Navy.

She had edged to within a few miles of the Confederate stronghold at Vicksburg, but no rebel forces had yet appeared to oppose her. And even if there should be an attack from the banks of the river, the *Cairo*'s 160 officers and men were confident that the ship would steam on undaunted.

The ship's sides were built of oak up to two feet thick, and every square foot was coated with iron. In some places the armor coating was two-and-a-half inches thick.

Her guns were shielded behind a deck house that ran almost the full length of the ship. All four sides of the house had sloping walls that would deflect any cannon

A floating fortress, the Cairo *steamed ever closer to the Confederate fortress at Vicksburg.*

ball and make rebels' bullets bounce off like rain on a roof. On top of the deck house, the small bridge was also shielded behind sloping walls of thick oak and iron.

On December 12, 1862, this juggernaut began steaming down the Yazoo, moving closer to Vicksburg. The Union strategy was to enter the Mississippi and use the *Cairo* as the spearhead of an assault force that would land troops south of Vicksburg. Then a north-south pincher attack could be launched against the fortress. Vicksburg was sure to fall, and when it did, the North would control the Mississippi all the way to New Orleans.

The Union strategy makers had good cause to put their trust in the *Cairo*. In March of the same year, the *Merrimac,* a similar ironclad that had been captured and refitted by the Confederates, had almost broken the Union blockade of Hampton Roads in Chesapeake Bay. In one day the *Merrimac* sent several wooden ships of the blockading fleet to the bottom, but when the ironside returned the second day to finish the havoc, she was stopped by a single vessel—the *Monitor.*

The *Merrimac* and the *Monitor,* a flat-decked ironside armed with a two-gun turret, pounded each other with shells, but neither ship suffered serious damage. In the end, however, the *Merrimac* had to retire, giving up her attempt to break the blockade. Just the same, the battle showed that an ironside was a match for any ship, even another ironside. And on the Mississippi, the Confederates had no ironside to oppose the *Cairo*.

Yet the *Cairo* was steaming to her doom.

The Confederate defenders, well aware of the Union strategy and the importance of thwarting it, had taken a

Vicksburg, at the junction of the Mississippi and the Yazoo, blocked Union access to New Orleans and the sea.

desperate gamble. They had decided to rely on a weapon yet untested in warfare—the electrical mine.

Under the cover of night, Rebel swimmers had mined Yazoo with these new devices. They were hastily made—simply bottles filled with powder and anchored in the channel, beneath the surface of the muddy river. Copper lines led to the shore where an electrical charge would provide the spark for detonation.

It was late in the morning when the *Cairo* was struck with a deafening blast. A gush of spray rose at her bow. The ship shuddered. For a time no one on board could guess what had happened. Soon, however, it became obvious that she had been holed. Water poured into her, and the pumps, working at full power could not keep ahead of the torrent. The *Cairo* began to settle in the river.

Fortunately, another Union ship steamed alongside to rescue the crew. The deck was well under when the final man jumped to safety. Then at 11:30 A.M. the ironside settled to the muddy bottom of the Yazoo.

In his diary, a cabin boy described the disaster:

"We moved off just in time to escape being swallowed up in the seething cauldron of foaming waters. Nothing of the *Cairo* could be seen twelve minutes after the first explosion, excepting the tops of the smokestacks and the flagstaff from which still floated above the troubled waters the sacred banner of our country."

The loss of the *Cairo* delayed the Vicksburg campaign. Not until July 4, 1863, did the fortress fall.

Union engineers tried several times to raise the ship, but it was a hopeless task. A large hole had been blown in her bow, and the ship's armor made her so heavy that no hoisting rig was strong enough to raise her. She was abandoned, and after the currents swept away her stacks and her masts, her position was lost.

For almost a century, this relic of the Civil War was all but forgotten.

Other famous ironsides fared no better. When the Confederate armies retreated from the Chesapeake, the *Merrimac* was run aground and burned. A tangled heap of scrap iron was all that remained of her.

Then on December 31, 1862, just nineteen days after the loss of the *Cairo,* the *Monitor* swamped in a storm and went down off Cape Hatteras with the loss of sixteen men.

Naval construction all but ceased after the war. All existing ironsides were scrapped, and when nations began building warships again, all-steel ships replaced wooden ships with iron armor. Thus no sample of the unique ironsides remained for historians to study and examine.

Was there a remedy for this situation? Edwin Bearse thought there just might be. In 1956, Bearse, a historian for the National Park Service, decided to find the *Cairo.* A student of the Civil War, he had studied all the records of the Vicksburg campaign and he had a general idea where the *Cairo* had gone down.

Bearse had also examined many oak timbers that had been recovered over the years along the banks of the Yazoo and the lower Mississippi. Finders of the timbers believed that they had come from the *Cairo,* but Bearse concluded that this was not so. He believed that the *Cairo* was still in one piece hidden beneath the muddy water.

Without funds for sophisticated metal detecting equipment Bearse decided to conduct his search with nothing more than a cheap compass purchased in a surplus store. He and two friends, M. D. Jacks, a riverman working for the park service, and Warren Grabau, a government geologist, started down the Yazoo in Jacks's small boat in November of 1956.

They kept a close eye on the compass. Once the needle swung slightly away from magnetic north. The three men decided the deviation was too slight to be worthy of immediate investigation, but they took note of a tree that grew near the spot for future reference.

Then for a long time the needle remained steady, but soon after they had drifted into what Bearse figured would be the most promising section of the river, the compass needle swung abruptly. It turned a full 180 degrees, pointing to something that clearly was a large magnetic attraction.

Using an iron rod to probe the bottom and following the course of the needle they worked their way across the current. Suddenly, the rod clanged on metal. They had found the *Cairo*.

Jubilantly they continued probing to determine the full extent of the ship. There could be no doubt. It was the ironside and in some places she lay no more than six feet below the surface.

Although Bearse, Jacks, and Grabau had achieved their immediate goal, their hopes of raising the ship received a setback when they began to figure the cost of the undertaking. It would take heavy salvaging equipment and a great deal of money. For a long time attempts to spark interest were disappointing, but in 1959 James Hart and Ken Parks, two Mississippi skin divers, offered to examine the wreck.

The divers faced a difficult job. The silty water forced them to explore the ship almost entirely by touch, but they managed to attach buoy lines to several key points. Next they used a water jet to remove great heaps of sand from the pilot house.

With the sand cleared out, relics of the Civil War were exposed. Hart and Parks brought up a mixed collection—

several medicine bottles, swords, a revolver, a wash bowl, a pitcher, a soap dish, a tub, a mirror, a can of shoe polish, and a folding chair.

Next the divers explored the ship's blacksmith shop and recovered hammers, drilling bits, chisels, a vise, and an anvil.

These finds prompted public interest and funds for a salvage effort. In 1960, the Anderson-Tully Lumber Company lent a huge crane for the operation, but its one-inch steel cables were not big enough for the strain of lifting the heavy hull. After snapping several cables, the salvagers settled for the prize of the pilot house, but even it was not broken free without a great deal of effort.

But the raising of the pilot house, the like of which had not been seen for almost a century, proved to be well worth the struggle. The State of Mississippi gave its support to the salvage operation, and helmeted divers provided by the U.S. Navy went to work airlifting sand from the decks and bringing up guns and other relics. The plan was to lighten the ship as much as possible and then try to raise the entire hull with pontoons.

The pontoons were to be sunk on either side of the hulk, and after being linked to it with stout cables, they would be pumped out, lifting *Cairo* as they rose. The plan, however, was scrapped after strong currents broke the pontoons' moorings and swept them downstream.

No serious further attempts were made until 1965, when a company headed by Captain W. J. Bisso brought four floating derricks with a combined lifting capacity of one thousand tons to the site. Tunnels were excavated beneath the *Cairo* so that seven stout cables up to three inches in diameter could be looped around the hull.

The derrick managed to lift the ironside off the bottom so that she could be carried upstream while still beneath the surface. A huge barge was then flooded and lowered into the hole where the Cairo had rested. The *Cairo* was then to be brought back and lowered on top of the barge, but the water level of the Yazoo lowered before this final step could be completed. The derricks strained to lift the *Cairo* higher out of the water, but the 176-foot ironside's own massive weight threatened to slice her to pieces, because as the cables tightened, they cut deeper and deeper into the hull.

At this point it was decided to give up further attempts at raising *Cairo* in one piece. So she was cut into three sections small enough for the derricks to handle.

The *Cairo,* now reconstructed, is on display in a special museum in Vicksburg, where scholars and the general public can inspect her and the many relics she carried. The ship proved to be a valuable time capsule. Her relics give new information on life aboard a Civil War ironclad, and inspection of the hull has revealed construction methods that could not be learned from study of the documents of the day.

There is another ironclad hidden by the sea. The *Monitor* lies beneath 230 feet of water seventeen miles southeast of Cape Hatteras. Located in 1973 by a Duke University research vessel, the ironclad has since been the focus of several diving expeditions. She has been photographed by both still and television cameras, which have provided scholars with valuable data on her construction, but salvage experts have concluded that currents are too tricky and the water is too deep to attempt raising her.

So the *Cairo,* thanks to river archeology, stands today as the only ironclad on public display, a unique ship from a bygone era.

PART III

The Seven Seas

Chapter Nine

~~~~~~~~~~~~~~~~~~~~~~~~~~~~

Fight or Die

Three centuries ago, the maritime powers of the world were struggling for control of the lucrative trade with the East Indies, a trade that brought spices, silks, fine porcelain, precious gems, and other luxury items to the capitals of Europe.

One successful voyage could make a fortune for a bold merchant, but the risks were high.

The trade route led down into the storm-lashed South Atlantic, around the horn of Africa and then far east to thread through the treacherous reefs and islands of Indonesia. Navigation was difficult and storms could strike with little warning. But the greatest danger rose from the rivalry between trading nations. All ships sailed armed and with orders to shoot first and arbitrate later.

There was no room for arbitration between the Dutch and the Portuguese, the bitterest rivals in the competition for eastern trade. Neither side in this rivalry gave mercy. And mercy was never asked. It was fight or die.

Thus Dom Geronimo de Almeida, captain in charge

of two Portuguese ships, knew he faced a fight the moment he spotted the Dutch flags. The flags flew from four ships. De Almeida was outnumbered two to one. And even worse, he lay at anchor with no time to hoist sail and maneuver into a position of advantage.

The year was 1613. The place was James Bay at the tiny island of St. Helena far out in the South Atlantic. St. Helena, later to be Napoleon's home of exile, was a convenient stopping place for both outbound and home-bound ships of the Eastern trade. In this sheltered place, crews could refit and repair storm damage and take on water and provisions with little risk.

The only danger was enemy guns, guns that now threatened.

Determined to give battle, de Almeida prepared his ships quickly. As the big Dutch East Indiamen sailed to the attack, the Portuguese crews cleared their decks and rolled guns into position. When their flags ran to their mastheads, the Portuguese were ready.

It was soon clear, from their low position in the water, that the Dutch ships were homeward bound, heavy with cargo, and not as maneuverable as they might have been if lightly laden. And they bore straight down on the anchored ships in a show of might and confidence. Undoubtedly the Dutch thought it was a great piece of luck to sail into James Bay and find two Portuguese ships practically waiting to be either sunk or captured.

But the Dutch had not reckoned on the accuracy of the Portuguese gunners. Cool and well-disciplined, the men on the anchored ships knew that their only hope lay in good marksmanship. And today their aim was true. First to open fire, their broadsides took immediate effect.

Portuguese shot shattered the Dutch fleet before it could close for action. The largest ship, leader of the

Dutch attack, shook with a deafening explosion, settled by the stern, and sank. Another Dutch ship suffered such severe damage to her forecastle that she was forced to withdraw. The remaining two ships, also badly battered, were not up to continuing a fight that had been quickly reduced to even odds. They too withdrew, conceding victory to the Portuguese.

The Portuguese cheered their victory as the Dutch retreated below the horizon. Captain de Almeida went to his cabin to enter his description of the battle in the ship's log. It gave him particular satisfaction to write that one of the cursed Dutch ships had "gone down with all its cargo."

In our own century, the same phrase can quicken the heart of any underwater adventurer. Robert Sténuit of Belgium was no exception. He had devoted many years to the search and examination of Spanish wrecks in the Caribbean, and he had written many magazine articles about these adventures, but in the 1970s he turned his full attention to James Bay.

He began by reading eyewitness accounts and official reports of the battle by both the Dutch and the Portuguese. The ship that sank was called *Witte Leeuw,* Dutch for White Lion. She had been loaded with exotic goods, rare porcelain, and spices, and she carried a fortune in diamonds—1,311 of them, according to the shipping records.

But Sténuit was drawn by more than treasure. He knew that few other Dutch East Indiamen had been investigated, and they had been wrecked on the outbound journey. They carried silver bullion and factory goods from Europe to be used in trade for products of the Orient. The wreck at St. Helena contained an entirely different cargo. And the battle in James Bay occurred at a fascinating time in history. Not only were West and East beginning to trade goods, but they were also beginning to exchange traditions of art, literature, religion, and philosophy.

Surely, the wreck of the *Witte Leeuw* was worth a thorough search.

In 1975, with his research completed, Sténuit received support for a search from Henri Delauze, president of a French underwater engineering company, and the National Geographic Society. Then he alerted some well-chosen friends who had been with him on previous expeditions. He asked Michel Tavernier, Alain Fink, Louis Gorsse, and Michel Gangloff to be ready to go to St. Helena if needed. The veteran divers agreed.

St. Helena has long been a British colony, and Sir Thomas Oates, the governor, welcomed Sténuit and promised government assistance in the search for the *Witte Leeuw*.

Despite his extensive research, Sténuit had found few clues that would help him locate the wreck. But modern sailing directions for James Bay warned of two spots where anchors are likely to foul on underwater obstructions. Could one of these spots mark the remains of the ship?

In his preliminary dives, Sténuit was unable to answer this question, but he did make some encouraging discoveries. The muddy bottom of the bay was level, currents were slight, and the water was so clear that he could see objects on the sea floor at a distance of eighty feet. Finding a sunken East Indiaman should be fairly easy.

Sténuit went back to Europe and rounded up his divers. He also lined up a side-scanning sonar instrument that should hasten the search. It would arrive soon after the divers reached St. Helena.

Diving began on a bright morning in June, 1976. The men went down in pairs to sweep the bottom in paral-

lel paths. They were linked by an eighty-foot nylon cord
to help them maintain proper separation. In this manner,
they could follow a grid pattern in their search that would
cover the entire bottom of the bay if necessary.

They first investigated one of the foul anchorage
areas and were still working there on the third day when
Sténuit and his diving partner, Michel Gangloff, made a
discovery in 110 feet of water. Actually, it was Gangloff
who made the initial find. He gave three tugs on the nylon
cord to bring Sténuit over and inspect a large cannon,
heavily encrusted and partially buried in the mud. The
cannon seemed to be cast in iron. Soon three more cannons were found, and then not far off, two more for a
total of six cannons, all too heavily encrusted to be identified.

When their diving time ran out, Sténuit and Gangloff
rose in stages to the surface. Sténuit instructed the next
team, Alain Fink and Louis Gorsse, to search the area
carefully for any relics that might give some idea of age.
Sténuit suspected that the guns had either been jettisoned
from a more recent ship that was trying to lighten itself
before facing a long sea voyage or else marked the sinking
of a more recent vessel. His reasoning was based on his
knowledge that brass not iron was used to make cannons
when the *Witte Leeuw* went down.

After an extensive search, the only relics that divers
could find in the area were jugs and bottles dating back
only to the eighteenth century. This seemed to confirm
that the cannons had arrived in James Bay long after the
Witte Leeuw sank. The site had to be explored more fully,
but at this point, the sonar gear arrived under the care of
engineer Dick Bishop who was ready to start using it. It
was time to make a full scan of the bay.

For ten hours each day, crowded in a small boat, the

searchers motored back and forth across the surface while
Bishop gradually put together a detailed profile of the
bottom. Oil drums, anchors, an old barge, and the remains
of several ships showed up in the scanner, but there was
nothing that suggested the wreck of an East Indiaman.

The divers checked everything that gave the slightest
possibility of being the *Witte Leeuw,* but the debris was
always of the wrong type and age to mark the Dutch ship.
When the sonar search was finished, the six cannons remained the most promising relics on the floor of James
Bay. The divers decided that the only thing to do was
bring one of the cannons up and take a close look at it.

Sténuit's research had revealed that the ship had carried about thirty cannons, and if it sank quickly as the
records indicated, there would be far more than just six
cannons on the muddy floor of the bay. But perhaps the
records were wrong.

It took two days of work with the air lift to remove
enough mud around one of the cannons to strap a heavy
line around it. Gorsse then went down with three neoprene bags and some extra air tanks. The bags were firmly
fastened to the line and then they were filled with air.
The air bags pulled the cannon from its muddy resting
place. The old weapon rose, trailing a cloud of muddy
water.

Then both the bags and the cannon, still beneath the
surface, were towed to a bayside dock where a crane
plucked the cannon out of the water. Cleaning and inspection began at once.

Immediately the divers discovered that the cannon
was made of brass, not iron, but an unusually heavy
layer of encrustations delayed identification. Mixed in
with the metal oxides covering the weapon was a substance that could not at once be identified. Finally, after

Air balloons lift an old cannon from the floor of St. Helena's James Bay to open a new venture in discovery.

much careful chipping, Sténuit exposed the letters of an inscription—REENICHDE. The Dutch words for the United East India Company were De Vereenichde Oost-Indig Comp. The *Witte Leeuw* had been found! No other confirmation was needed, but when it was discovered that the odd substance mixed in with the encrusting oxides was pepper, thousands of kernels of the unground stuff that had survived centuries of immersion, there could be no doubt. The *Witte Leeuw*'s cargo had included 15,171 bags of pepper.

When diving resumed, however, Sténuit was still puzzled. If the *Witte Leeuw* had carried thirty guns, why were there just six in this spot? A wide area of search was ordered, and before long another gun was found about seventy feet from the others. Then still another was discovered eighty feet away in an entirely different direction. It seemed clear now that the accounts of the battle were wrong. The ship had not gone down at once. Instead, she had either broken up on the surface or else she had drifted for a time, spilling her heavy guns across the bottom before she sank.

Using a diving platform supported by empty oil drums, the divers put an air lift to work in the area where the six cannons had been found. At first the lift brought up a mixed lot of refuse—beer bottles, old shoes, tin cans, and pieces of broken crockery, all discarded from recent ships. There was some excitement when bones appeared in the stream of mud, but these proved to be goat bones that were thrown into the bay by some latter day sea cook.

But finally, after the pump intake had excavated to a depth of ten feet below the floor of the bay, porcelain began to come up with the rubbish. These were fragments of Ming China that were old enough and fine enough to be part of the *Witte Leeuw*'s cargo.

Divers cleared away the pottery fragments to find a section of deck planking. Sténuit believed that boring worms had destroyed most of the wood of the wreck, but this section of deck, probably from the lower part of the ship, had been sunk so deeply in mud that the worms could not reach it.

After lifting the wood away carefully, the divers came upon ship's ballast made up of river stones, old bricks, and chunks of lead. Continuing to use the air lift, divers then began expanding the excavation. They soon dug into pepper, a thick deposit of the spice, two yards deep in some places. After several days, with the pepper finally cleared away, the divers found a treasure in porcelain.

At first the men's fingers picked broken fragments out of the mud, but then whole vessels appeared. Unblemished bowls and dishes, masterpieces of oriental craftsmanship, rose one after the other in the tender care of the veteran divers. On the surface, the growing collection was viewed with silent admiration.

The pieces were not only beautifully shaped but they were also decorated with a rich blue glaze in patterns unmatched in form and grace. Many decorations followed a floral motif, but the Ming artist took equal delight in depicting butterflies, grasshoppers, and frogs. Some designs

Rare samples of blue and white, Chinese porcelain were preserved beneath a thick cargo of pepper.

An elephant teapot, slightly chipped at the top, was designed to pour twin jets through its tusks.

were whimsical. One teapot, shaped like an elephant, spouted twin jets through its tusks when poured.

Sténuit, who knew the history of oriental porcelain, recognized the discoveries as products of the late sixteenth and early seventeenth centuries. Most of the pieces, he believed had been made in Chingtechen, a pottery center in China's southern province. Unbroken ware of this style and era was extremely rare. Sténuit estimated the value of some pieces at $1,000. And in the hands of scholars, the unbroken pieces, firmly dated at no later than 1613 when the *Witte Leeuw* went down, would be of immeasurable value in identifying and dating broken fragments that had been found elsewhere.

At one time, Ming pottery was extremely popular in European markets and highly prized in European homes. It was in such high demand that Dutch potters learned to prepare an oxide of cobalt that would match the blue glaze, and began producing a domestic blue and white porcelain. Known as delftware, it established a tradition of high quality that has lasted into our own century.

The porcelain collected from the bottom of James
Bay was by itself enough to fully justify the expedition,
but the divers hoped to find much more, particularly the
Witte Leeuw's diamonds. They did indeed find more relics
—a silver boatswain's whistle, brass oil lamps, plain table-
ware that was probably used by the crew, and two bow-
chaser cannons, each weighing more than two tons. The
cannons, made in Amsterdam, bore the maker's name
and date: *Henricus Mevrs me fecit 1604.*

Among the most curious finds were eggs that had
survived the battle and the sinking without a crack. The
divers also brought up an extensive collection of seashells
that had been gathered from the Indonesian coast, probably by a member of the ship's company. Did some Dutch
sailor fill his idle hours beachcombing while waiting to
sail again? It seemed likely.

But despite the variety of interesting finds, not a
single diamond came to light.

Sténuit speculated that the diamonds had probably
been stowed away securely in the captain's cabin in the
aft section of the ship, the section that reportedly split off
and drifted away after an explosion. But several exploratory excavations with the air lift failed to locate any sign
of the aft section.

So, after seven months in James Bay, the divers
packed their gear and helped crate all the relics that had
been recovered. Then they headed home to Europe. The
relics, including the beautiful porcelains, were shipped to
the Rijksmuseum in Amsterdam, Holland, where they are
now on display with other treasures from the era of East
Indian trade.

Sténuit went home fully intending to return to St.
Helena and continue his search for the missing section of
Witte Leeuw, but soon after he settled into his home in

Brussels, Belgium, he received a letter that changed his mind.

Actually, there were two letters, one from Charles Kendall, the government secretary on St. Helena, who enclosed the second letter written by a South African who had studied the East Indian trade.

In his research, the South African had come across a document that Sténuit had never seen. It gave an eyewitness account of the battle written by an English officer whose ship had been anchored near the Portuguese ships.

The officer reported that the *Witte Leeuw* "blew up all in pieces, the after part of her, and so sunke presently." It was the officer's assumption that a spark had ignited the ship's store of powder.

Sténuit realized at last that he and his divers had been unable to locate the aft section of the ship simply because it no longer existed. It had been shattered to splinters.

So he decided that his search was over, that the expedition had found all that could be feasibly recovered. True, a fortune in diamonds scattered across the muddy bottom of James Bay, but today Sténuit is satisfied, quite content to let some other hardy adventurers of the deep take up the quest for *Witte Leeuw*'s diamonds.

Chapter Ten

~~~~~~~~~~~~~~~~

The Pride
of Sweden

She was a floating fortress. Her three gun decks were armed with a total of forty-eight heavy cannons. In addition she carried six howitzers and several smaller guns. The weight of her cannons alone was eighty tons, and she carried a full load of ammunition, plus provisions for a hundred and forty sailors and about three hundred marines. Her manifest listed nine hundred cases of food and twelve hundred barrels of beer.

The *Vasa*, pride of Sweden's navy, sailed on her maiden voyage on Sunday, August 10, 1628.

The three-master was the biggest of four new warships built to guard the Baltic Sea. And at the time, threat to this sea, a vital waterway for Sweden, was very real.

The Thirty Years' War had been raging across Europe since 1611, and Sweden's enemies—the House of Hapsburg, Bavaria, and their Catholic allies—had recently been winning all the important battles.

Under King Gustaf Adolf, Sweden stood as a bastion of Protestantism, but across the Baltic, all of western Germany had been overrun by Catholic forces under the leadership of Albrecht von Wallenstein and other brilliant generals. Wallenstein's next logical goal was to wrest control of the Baltic from Sweden.

Knowing this, Gustaf Adolf ordered Henrik Hyberrsson, a Dutch shipbuilder, to design four new ships. Their construction began in 1625.

The *Vasa* was to be the ultimate achievement in shipbuilding art. She would be awesome, mighty, and beautiful. The best woodcarvers in the land were hired to ornament her with figures. When lifted, the underside of each gun port cover would display the head of a fierce lion, and a lion would also snarl at her bow as a royal figurehead.

With pride, the people of Stockholm watched her being built. Her hull was 150 feet long, and her tallest mast peaked 180 feet above her keel. It topped the buildings and most of the nearby church steeples. She was finally launched in 1627, but it took several months to outfit and rig her. The work was done in front of the palace where Gustaf Adolf could watch the daily progress. The men could not work fast enough to please him, and his impatience was justified. Catholic forces now controlled all of Germany and had begun to collect a fleet to challenge Sweden for dominance in the Baltic.

Well before *Vasa* was ready to sail, her role was planned. She was to sail for Älvsnabben, an island off the coast south from Stockholm, where she was to await the king's orders. From the island she could sail at once to attack or to a position of defense as the situation might dictate.

August 10 dawned warm and clear with just a few dark clouds in the distance to give a hint of threatening weather. It was a good day for sailing and a perfect day for a festival.

All of Stockholm, joined by thousands of farm families from the surrounding countryside, had turned out to witness the event. Many lucky enough to have relatives on the ship were allowed aboard to sail as far as Älvsnabben.

The ship left the dock as thousands lining the wharf and clinging to rooftops cheered and waved banners. As church bells rang, the ship eased out to the smooth waters of Mälar Lake under four reefed sails. A flag of Sweden fluttered from each mast.

Soon after the *Vasa* nosed toward Stockholm Ström, the channel that leads from Mälar Lake to the Baltic, Captain Sofring Hansson ordered a farewell salute. The burst of smoke and the boom of the guns was answered by a renewed wave of cheering from the festive crowd at the docks.

And the cheering continued as the mighty ship sailed slowly into the Ström. Her voyage had begun.

Then, without warning, a strong gust blew down from the nearby mountains. The sails filled abruptly and the ship heeled dangerously. The deck was so crowded that it was hard to find a handhold to keep from sliding to the lee rail. Experienced seamen assured the frightened visitors that the ship would soon right itself, but the wind strengthened and the *Vasa* continued to lean. Captain Hansson ordered the sails cut loose. But even with the canvas flapping wildly in the gale, the ship would not come back to an even keel.

Her destination was Alvsnabben Island, but the Vasa *barely cleared her home port before disaster struck.*

Ordnance Master Erik Jonnsson dashed below and ordered the gunners to begin winching the cannons on the leeward side up to windward. The shift might have countered the force of the wind, but it was too late. The lower cannon ports, already underwater, gave entry to torrents of green sea. The *Vasa* settled and listed even more. Soon her lee rail was under, and then before the horrified eyes of the spectators, she sank from sight.

A fleet of rescue boats rushed to the scene, but they were unable to save all the *Vasa*'s people. Fifty souls were lost with the ship.

Church bells that began the day with peals of joy, now tolled in the evening with mournful notes.

A royal investigation began at once. The ship's officers, including Captain Hansson, were arrested. The directors of the boatyard were also jailed. Designer Henrik Hybertsson escaped arrest only because he had died before his ship was finished.

The day after the tragedy, the Swedish parliament convened a court-martial inquiry. Why had the ship sunk? No one could give the answer. Had it been loaded improperly with too much weight above the waterline or was the ship's design at fault?

It was hard to question the design because the king himself had given the plans his enthusiastic endorsement. The court finally adjourned without fixing the blame on any individual, but it is suspected today that the huge ship with her many cannons and crowded decks was most likely topheavy, unable to right herself in the gust.

Meanwhile, three days after the sinking, Jan Bulmer received permission from the Swedish parliament to salvage the *Vasa*. Bulmer, an engineer from the English court who was visiting in Stockholm, witnessed the tragedy. He thought it was important to begin salvage work while the tips of the great ship's mast still showed above the surface to mark her position.

But Bulmer did not have a clear plan of salvage. The masts showed that the vessel had settled to the bottom at an angle with her deck about ninety feet below the surface. Bulmer decided that the first thing to do was try to right the ship. The divers he hired went down without breathing gear or protective suits and tied stout ropes to the masts. The ropes were strung to shore and hitched to horses. After a great deal of strain on both horses and harness, the ship was pulled to an even keel. What next?

The English engineer had no answer. He eventually gave up, the first of several to be frustrated by the task.

In the fall of 1628, the Swedish navy, using chains and hooks, managed to snag the sunken ship in several spots on her superstructure and gun ports, but when a lift was attempted, hooks bent and chains snapped. Admiral Klas Fleming reported that the *Vasa* was too heavy to be raised in this manner.

A series of fortune seekers followed, but after tearing away much of the superstructure and leaving behind an array of snagged hooks and anchors, all would-be salvagers reached the same conclusion. Conventional methods would not work on the *Vasa*.

In 1663, thirty-five years after the tragedy, Hans Albrekt von Treileben, a former colonel in the Swedish army, and Andreas Peckell, a German salvage expert, made an attempt with their invention—a diving bell.

The two men also had a realistic plan. They would not try to raise the huge ship, only her cannons, which could be melted down for the valuable bronze. Preparatory work, including removal of deck planking, took a full year, but in the spring of 1664 the first cannon came to the surface.

The diver in the bell, using nothing more than hooks and tongs, had to snare each cannon, fix a hoisting rope to it, and make sure that it cleared the ship's wreckage when lifted. Cannons salvaged from the lower deck were hauled out through the gun ports. Such work would challenge the patience of a modern day skin diver, but in three years, Peckell and Treileben managed to raise fifty cannons from the *Vasa*. On today's bronze market, their price would be worth $125,000. Although they left many inaccessible cannons below, their effort was deemed a remarkable success.

But it seemed that nothing more could be done. For almost three centuries, the *Vasa* lay undisturbed and virtually forgotten. And with her masts broken and washed away, her position was soon lost.

Probably little more thought would ever have been given to the crown ship if Anders Franzen had not had a lifelong dream. The son of an amateur historian, Franzen's youth had been filled with tales of Sweden's great past, particularly of the days when she was a naval power. What had become of the tall ships? All were gone. Some had sunk, and the rest had rotted away with age.

Young Franzen yearned to see at least one of these ships, and finding one became his special dream.

In 1920, while he was still a young man, he heard news of an exciting discovery. Near the island of Viksten not far from Stockholm, after a fisherman's anchor snagged for a second time at the same spot, a diver went down to discover the remains of a large wooden vessel. The Swedish government paid a $12,500 reward for the discovery and for the seven ornate bronze cannons that were raised from the wreck. The cannons were put on display in the Stockholm Marine Historical Museum, and when Anders Franzen saw the relics he became more determined than ever to make his dream come true.

Franzen joined the Royal Swedish Navy and devoted much of his military career to the development of improved oils and fuels for marine engines. In his spare time, he became an expert in his country's maritime history. He read hundreds of old documents and began charting the general location of reported wrecks. Then, in 1939, he made an important discovery that gave him great encouragement.

It was during a cruise along the west coast of Sweden outside the Baltic Sea. Franzen fished a few pieces of wood

out of the ocean and was surprised to see how badly rid-
dled they were by shipworms. The wood he had recovered
in the Baltic had been in much better condition with no
sign of worms. He realized that shipworms were not able
to thrive in the Baltic because it had a lower salt content
than most of the world's oceans. Thus any wooden ship
that had sunk in the Baltic would be in much better condition than ships sunk elsewhere. Fortunately, nearly all of
the old ships that concerned him had gone down in the
Baltic.

A few years later, the development of scuba diving
gear gave Franzen added hope. The new gear meant that
diving in search of wrecks would not be nearly as expensive
as he feared. In fact, it could be done by amateurs, men and
women who were as enthusiastic about discovering the
past as he was. Franzen was among the first to purchase an
Aqualung, and before long some of his friends acquired
the gear.

Meanwhile, Franzen continued his studies of the
dusty documents. He poured over ship's logs and old
charts. He also listened to the stories that veteran seamen
told, stories that had been passed on through generations.
After hours of work, Franzen had a list of fifty ships that
had gone down along the Swedish coast. From this list,
he selected twelve that seemed both accessible and promising. His list included the *Vasa,* but after lengthy talks with
specialists at the Marine Historical Museum, Franzen
picked *Riksäpplet* as the most promising.

A Swedish navy ship, it had been wrecked in 1676
when a storm drove it onto rocks in the Bay of Dalarö
southeast of Stockholm. The rocks punched a hole in the
oak hull and the ship had gone down in forty-eight feet
of water, a depth that presented little difficulty to frogmen.

But it took only a few dives to determine that centuries of storm and drifting ice had destroyed most of the

remains. After Franzen and his friends found a few scattered timbers and planks, they concluded that the choicest pieces of oak had been taken long ago by local salvagers. Just the same, what wood the divers did find confirmed Franzen's theory that the Baltic Sea is kind to submerged wood. The oak was blackened, but there was no worm damage.

Shortly after investigating the remains of *Riksäpplet* and while he was still pondering his next step, Franzen met Mils Ahnlund, a professor of history who had devoted much of his long career to the study of naval records. It was a lucky meeting. Franzen respected the scholar's vast knowledge, and Ahnlund liked the younger man's enthusiasm. The professor urged Franzen to give his full attention to the *Vasa,* a ship that had gone down in protected waters.

Franzen went back to the archives and studied every piece of information he could find on the crown ship, including the reports of early salvage attempts. Nothing in the record gave the precise location of the sinking, but in the summer of 1954 Franzen began his search. He rented a boat at Stockholm harbor, loaded it with cables, lines and hooks and sailed out into Stockholm Ström.

He had to work from the surface because the waters of the Ström were far too muddy to search by diving. Franzen's hooks pulled up rusty stoves, old bedsteads, bicycles, discarded Christmas trees, and dead cats. There was no sign of a ship.

He went out again in the summer of 1955, exploring the Ström with sonar and then with a bottom sounding tool he had invented, a rocket-shaped tube that brought up samples of the sea floor.

Off the town of Beckholmsudden, his sonar indicated a mound in the floor of the Ström, but he did not investi-

gate it because local seamen told him that rock blasted
from the excavation for a drydock had been dumped in
that place. So winter ice closed in once more, and Franzen
had still not located the *Vasa*.

He returned to the archives for more research. This
time, his persistence was rewarded. He came upon a document he had not seen before, a letter from the Swedish
parliament addressed to King Gustaf Adolf. It was dated
August 12, 1628, just two days after the *Vasa* sank. The
report said: "And on that fateful Sunday which was the
tenth day of this month, the *Vasa* set sail. But it happened
that she got no further than Beckholmsudden, where she
sank to the bottom with cannon and all else, and lies in
eighteen fathoms." The submerged hill off Beckholmsudden must be investigated.

After waiting impatiently through the winter,
Franzen went to work again in the summer of 1956. He
used his sounding gear to make probes into the hill. The
first probe brought up a piece of black oak. He moved a
few feet and tried again. More oak. After taking many
soundings at several different locations he knew that little
more than 100 feet down was a wooden object some 150
feet long and several feet wide. The *Vasa!*

The next step was to round up divers. Franzen was
sure that frogmen would not be of much use in the muddy
water. He would have to have a crew of helmeted divers,
and this meant expensive professionals. He had no money
for such divers, but as usual Franzen solved the problem.

He went to the commander of the Swedish navy's diving school and suggested that the school use the waters of
the Ström for a training ground where the wreckage of an
old ship would provide interest for the student divers.
The commander liked the idea, and before long the
school's diving boat was chugging into the Ström.

Edvin Fälting, a veteran diver, was the first to go down. Franzen kept contact with him over the diving phone. After the first few feet, underwater visibility dropped to zero, and when Fälting sank up to his chest in the bottom mud, he gave a discouraging report. Nothing but thick mud. A disheartened Franzen told Fälting to come back up.

But suddenly there was a startled shout from the diver. He had run into something solid. It felt like a wall of wood. After a few moments, the diver's voice crackled from the phone. "It's a big ship. No doubt about it."

He climbed the wall, feeling out rectangular openings that marked the gun ports. Then he stood on the *Vasa*'s deck amid a tangle of old salvage gear.

News of the discovery soon spread across Sweden. The *Vasa* had indeed been found, and she was in one piece. Was she worth raising? While the school divers continued exploring the ship, a committee was formed to investigate the possibilities of salvaging the ship intact. There was a great deal of public support for the project. The Neptune Salvage Company offered to raise the vessel without charge, and the navy said its divers would continue working on the project for the experience alone.

Just the same, the ambitious project would cost millions of dollars. The committee took on the job of raising funds. They also began considering methods for raising the hull. There were some odd suggestions.

One inventor proposed that the hull be filled with Ping-Pong balls until there were so many tiny capsules of air in her that she would rise to the surface. Another man suggested that the water inside the hull be frozen so that the ship would rise to the surface like an iceberg. But the committee decided to stick with more conventional methods.

After Franzen used samples of wood from the old hull to show that the oak retained sixty percent of its original strength, the committee decided it would be safe to use the cable and pontoon method. The plan was to lay cables under the *Vasa,* and lower pontoons on either side of her. After lashing the cables to the pontoons, air would slowly be pumped into them. As they rose, the old hull would rise with them. And if Franzen were correct and the wood was still sound, the cables would not cut into or crush the hull.

There was considerable doubt, however, that the plan would work. The *Vasa,* after all, weighed 700 tons. And the doubt, unfortunately, made it difficult to raise money. So with just enough to pay for the initial work, the divers got started. Their first job was to cut tunnels under the hull for six cables. An air lift and a water jet were both put to use, but tunneling proved far more difficult than anticipated. The loose mud around the sides of the hull kept collapsing. One diver was trapped in a cave-in and had to be dug free by the air lift. When all the loose mud was finally cleared, the divers faced hard clay. Boring through it was slow work even with a powerful water jet.

But the work brought an unsuspected bonus—statues. The crown ship had been decorated lavishly with ornate carvings in oak, linden, and pine. The sculpture work had been fastened to the hull with iron bolts. The bolts had rusted away, and statues had dropped into the mud all around the ship. Mud had sealed them so well from wear and decay that some of the statues still showed touches of gold paint when brought to the surface.

Done in the baroque style of the seventeenth century, many of the statues depicted figures from Greek mythology such as Hercules and Cerberus, the hound he conquered, and Nereus, the Greek god who could foresee

The symbol of royalty, a lion once snarled from the proud bow of the Vasa.

the future. King David holding a lyre, dragons, knights, and mermaids had also decorated the ship. There was a shield carved with the royal coat of arms, and out of mud near the bow of the *Vasa* came her figurehead, the snarling lion with threatening claws bared to all enemies. The fierce beast still glistened with traces of gold.

The carvings fascinated both historians and art specialists, and great care was taken to preserve the finds. Specialists cleaned them and then immersed them at once in a bath of polyethylene glycol, a waxy alcohol that dissolves in water. The glycol, soaking slowly into the wood, drives the water out and seals old wood. Had the waterlogged wood been allowed to dry in the air, shrinkage and cracking would have destroyed the beauty of the carvings.

Tunneling under the hull was completed in August, 1959. The next step was to bring the pontoons into position. Tugs of the Neptune Salvage Company towed the huge pontoons, *Oden* and *Frigg* (named for the leader of the old Norse gods and his wife) to the site and positioned them on either side of the submerged hull. Next, cables were run through the tunnels and rigged to cradle the *Vasa* between the two pontoons. Then they were flooded until their decks were awash. The cables were pulled taut and lashed down.

With their ports sealed again, the pontoons were slowly pumped dry so they again rose to their normal waterline. Workers on the fleet of boats surrounding the pontoons waited tensely as a diver went down to report the situation. Had the old hull lifted or had the strain been too much for her?

The diver's voice came up the phone line. "A foot and a half! Everything O.K." The *Vasa* had been raised off the bottom with no apparent damage.

The news brought jubilant shouts among the salvagers, but this was just the beginning. Tugs pushed the pontoons gently into shallower water until the *Vasa* rested on the bottom again. Then the pontoons were reflooded, the cables retightened, and the pumps restarted.

In the days that followed, this slow process was repeated again and again. After twenty-seven days, when the *Vasa* was still under forty-five feet of water, the work stopped. More money would be needed to complete the project.

During the winter of 1959–60, Crown Prince Bertil, an enthusiastic observer of the work, gave his energies and name to the fund raising effort. He took over leadership of the committee and persuaded the government officials to make substantial donations for the salvage fund. But engineering problems still remained.

The pontoons, now equipped with hydraulic winches to tighten the cables, would be able to lift the *Vasa* until her decks were awash, but because objects weigh more out of water than when immersed, the pontoons would not be able to raise the ship completely. The committee decided that the only solution was to make the old hull watertight and then pump water out of her so that she would attain some degree of buoyancy.

Divers went to work sealing gun ports and hatches and mending planks, but they soon found that many of the ship's nails were so badly rusted that they had to be replaced. It meant that thousands of new nails would have to be driven into the ship's sides. Pounding nails underwater is a slow, clumsy undertaking, but the work went ahead. It took months, but finally, after the last nail was pounded, the salvage pontoons were floated into position once again. It was April 14, 1961.

Inflatable rubber floats were attached to the hull's stern before the hydraulic winches on the pontoons went into action. This was because the stern of the *Vasa* was exceptionally heavy. The floats were needed to keep her rising on an even keel.

On April 24, as the winches slowly drew in the cables, the outline of the old warship gradually took shape beneath the murky surface. The stumps of the masts broke through the water first. Then vertical ends of the ship's ribs appeared, and soon the horizontal deck beams came into view.

Raised at last, the Vasa *revealed her secrets and became the focus of a massive preservation effort.*

Now it was time to turn on the big pumps. Churning out water at the rate of 7,500 gallons a minute, the pumps gradually lowered the level of water inside the *Vasa*. Ever so slowly, she rose higher from her watery grave.

Finally the hull was clear enough to slip her over a 170-foot-long, submerged pontoon. The pontoon was then given just enough buoyancy to support the old hull with gentle pressure from below. On May 4, the pontoon and its precious cargo were docked. The water level inside the *Vasa* stood at her upper gun deck, but once at the dock, it did not take long to pump the *Vasa* dry.

Now there was a rush of work. Men swarmed over her. Some had hoses that were kept in play constantly, soaking the old planks and timbers, which could not be allowed to dry quickly. Behind the hose crews, men came with plastic sheets, covering exposed parts of the hull. Then the experts came with liberal supplies of glycol.

While this work was in progress, the scientists and historians began a minute inspection of the ship. A jubilant Franzen accompanied them.

In some compartments, it was necessary to dredge away thick layers of mud, but when the clearing work was done, the scientists found relics of shipboard life just as it had been left more than three hundred years ago. Cooking pots, beer mugs, weapons, powder kegs, carpenter's tools, coins, and seamen's chests were all stowed in their appropriate compartments. One man even found a lump of rancid butter. In all, the *Vasa* yielded some ten thousand relics.

The remains of twelve victims of the sinking were found among the gun carriages. Their skeletons still bore the traces of their clothing. The typical outfit was a linen shirt under a vest knit of thick wool, which was covered in turn by a jacket with short, pleated coattails. Knit wool trousers apparently fastened below the knees. Footwear consisted of sewn linen stockings and sandals. One man

Museum visitors can now board the Vasa *and stand on decks that were once lined with cannons.*

carried a knife and money bag attached to his belt. Most men had a few coins in their pockets.

It took many more years to preserve and strengthen the ship and return the carvings to their proper spots before the *Vasa* was ready for public display. But now she stands in Stockholm for all to see, a relic of the past and a monument to one of the greatest achievements of underwater archeology.

Chapter Eleven

~~~~~~~~~~~~~~~~~~~~~~~~~~~

Viking Ships

Well before underwater archeology came of age, scholars knew more about Viking ships than any other ancient craft. The evolution of design and construction techniques could be traced through study of the vessels themselves, vessels found on dry land.

More than 400 ships built between 800 and 1100 A.D. survived to modern times either as entire vessels or in sections big enough to allow specialists to reconstruct them on paper if not as display models in museums.

We know that Viking shipbuilders used the shell-first method with frames added as strengthening members after the hull had been shaped with planks. The method was similar to early Mediterranean ship construction, but the Viking ships looked nothing like the short, broad cargo carriers built to the south.

The Viking boats were long and lean, and their planks overlapped so that the hulls could stand a good deal of pounding in rough seas. In heavy weather the planking could bend and twist and then spring back to position unharmed. The overlapping seams between the planks allowed this resiliency without the danger of serious leaks.

This "clinker" or overlap technique is still used for small boat construction and remains particularly popular in Scandinavian countries today.

Early boats of the Viking era were built with cleated planks. These cleats rose every few feet on the inner surface of each plank and were high enough to hold a rope lashing. The cleat ropes, tightened by twisting, drew the planks snuggly together and held the hull in shape. The cleat method avoided the necessity of boring holes through the planks and frames for a wooden peg or nail. But it took a great deal of time and wasted lots of wood to make cleated planks. All the wood between the cleats had to be laboriously chipped away. So despite a strong prejudice against boring holes through a ship's hull, the technique of pegging or nailing planks to frames eventually replaced cleat construction.

Thus cleated planks identify the early era and pegged or nailed planks identify the late era in Norse shipbuilding techniques. Other details, small but significant, help scholars place ships in both age and place of origin, but there was one great puzzle that troubled the experts.

From the records left by the Vikings and the peoples they traded with or raided, we know that long ocean voyages were common. The Vikings not only braved the storms of the North Sea, but they also crossed the North Atlantic to establish and maintain colonies in Iceland, Greenland, and the North American continent.

Today we are inclined to think that the Vikings, when not busy colonizing the New World, were hard at work pillaging the Old World. But the truth is that the Vikings were primarily merchants. They traveled for trade. True, peaceful commerce was occasionally interrupted by warfare, and the Vikings did establish a reputation as fierce fighters. But it was skill in trade that gave them maritime supremacy for more than three centuries.

What puzzled modern scholars was that out of all the old ships that had been recovered and preserved, no more than two or three seemed suited for trade. Certainly none were roomy enough and sturdy enough to cross the North Atlantic and land people and supplies in the New World.

One theory seemed to explain the puzzle. The ships that had survived through the centuries had been ceremonial ships, buried on dry land in keeping with Viking tradition and religion. While people of other cultures buried their dead with food, tools, and ornaments for use in the afterlife, the Vikings, when the importance of the deceased warranted, buried an entire ship. The ship, they believed, would carry the deceased on his or her journey into the afterlife.

Some ships, lightly constructed and richly carved, were apparently built especially for burial. Others were small coastal vessels that had probably been used by the deceased. Thus according to the theory, the burial tradition preserved a specific type of ship. It did not preserve the cargo ship, the working vessel of Viking trade.

But there was a conflicting theory long held by skeptical scholars. They said that the Vikings were overrated, that the tales of their long voyages of trade and colonization were exaggerations, and that sturdy Viking cargo ships had not been found simply because they never existed.

The conflict was resolved by an unusual excavation that mixed underwater archeology with dry-land techniques. And it was an excavation that was prompted by mistaken identity.

Since 1957, Olaf Olsen of the Danish National Mu-

seum had been searching for wrecks in Roskilde Fjord, an
inlet in the north shore of the island of Zealand. This
island, lying off the east coast of Denmark, had been an
important Viking stronghold. Its capital city of Lejre near
the head of the fjord and just west of the modern city
of Roskilde was a major Viking trade center.

The chief object of Olsen's quest was the "Ship of
Queen Margaret." Queen Margaret, who lived from 1363
to 1412, ruled over Norway, Sweden, and Denmark in a
rare era of unity. Among the many legends about her was

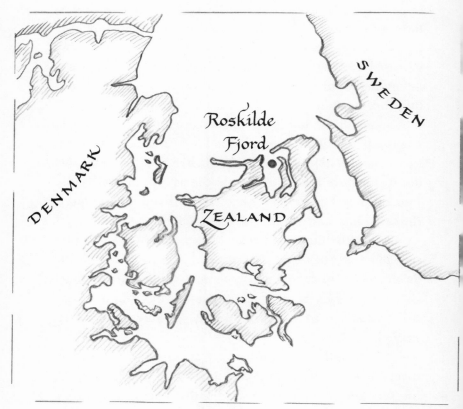

*A strategic harbor, Roskilde Fjord on the island of Zealand
faces the entrance to the Baltic Sea.*

the story that she once sank her own ship to block the entrance to the fjord against pirates who were intent on pillaging Lejre.

Fishermen led Olsen to the spot where they said that wreckage of the ship could be found. The water was three to nine feet deep, and the bottom was covered with large rocks, some weighing an estimated three hundred pounds. Olsen and his divers could not at first find any sign of a ship. Eventually, however, some old timbers were brought up. Again, thanks to the low salinity of the Baltic Sea, there was no damage from marine borers, but to Olsen's critical eye, the wood seemed to be at least 900 years old —too old to come from a ship of Queen Margaret's time.

This did not deter Olsen. On the contrary, he was all the more eager to investigate. In the shallow water, divers could work long hours without risking the bends. But there were special difficulties. The currents were strong, the water murky, and the heap of rocks made it very hard to determine just what lay below. The divers had to scrape mussels and seaweed from the rocks before they could begin mapping the site. But despite the problems, it soon became clear that not one but five different vessels had gone down. Had they been sunk by enemy action or deliberately scuttled?

The Danish National Museum financed a full investigation, and Olsen, joined by Ole Crumlin-Pedersen, also of the museum staff, planned their attack. A diving pontoon was anchored above the wrecks, and a wire, marked off in meters, was stretched across the site to serve as the measuring baseline. The divers began drawing plans of the wrecks on water resistant paper.

One fact became clear early in the expedition. The ships had been filled with rocks and sunk deliberately to form a blockade sometime in the tenth or eleventh cen-

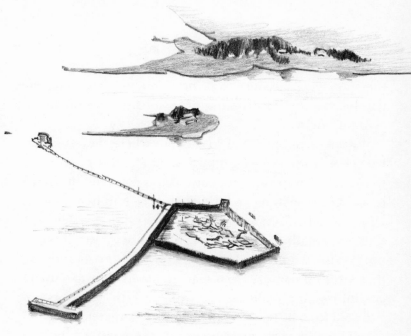

The five-sided coffer dam built around the wrecks enclosed one thousand six hundred square yards of sea floor.

tury A.D. And it was a very effective blockade, one that divers with even the best modern equipment would have difficulty removing.

After weighing the risks, Olsen and Crumlin-Pedersen haulted the diving operation. The excavation, they decided, would have to be converted to a dry-land dig. It was a startling idea, and an expensive one, too. Three years were spent raising money and planning the new operation.

Finally, in 1962, after several Danish foundations contributed funds and the contracting firm of Christiani and Nielsen volunteered its services, the unique project began.

The first step was to build a coffer dam around the ships. The five-sided enclosure made of sheet steel had to seal off sixteen hundred square yards of sea bottom.

When the coffer dam was at last completed, the pumps went to work, but the archeologists insisted that pumping be done slowly so that specialists would have plenty of time to clear and examine the old wood as it was exposed.

Gangplanks built over the wrecks made it possible to lift away the rocks and then work on the wrecks themselves without placing any unnecessary weight on the fragile wood. It was a strange excavation. The specialists soon found that knives and scrapers, common tools for dry land work, were not as effective in clearing mud as water jets. Still, the clearing and cleaning proceeded slowly. In fact, all phases of the operation were accomplished slowly and carefully.

After a hull was completely exposed and its timbers cleaned, it was mapped with stereoptic cameras. Then each timber was marked for identification, lifted from the site, and wrapped in air-tight plastic.

The timbers were next treated with polyethylene glycol, but the reconstruction phase of the project had to await the completion of a special museum at Roskilde to house the five ships. Just the same, the photos and photo maps already made clear to scholars that the wrecks made up a rare and very valuable collection. Here at last were samples of Viking cargo ships. Two of the wrecks fit this category without question, but they were not alike. The largest of the two was fifty-four feet long and fifteen feet wide. Its sturdy construction, with a keel and inner timbers of oak and planking of pine and linden, made it a heavy ship. It would have floated low in the water and won no prizes for speed, but it was a vessel fully capable of carrying large cargos on long voyages across open seas. Scholars identified it as a *knarr,* a ship mentioned in Viking reports of Atlantic crossings.

The second cargo ship, forty-four feet long and ten-and-a-half feet wide, was of lighter construction and used

Before reconstruction was complete, the sturdy timbers and large holding capacity of the knarr *showed she was a cargo vessel.*

most likely for coastal trade. Decked bow and stern, it had a large, open hold amidships for cargo. Although the main propulsion for both vessels was sail, the smaller boat had oar holes in its upper planking, one near the bow on the port side and two near the bow on the starboard side.

Scholars believe that the crew took up oars whenever it was necessary to maneuver in narrow waters. If it was indeed a coastal trade vessel, such rowing would often have been necessary.

The two cargo ships were not the largest recovered from Roskilde Fjord. That distinction goes to two warships, one of which had the amazing length of ninety-two feet. It could easily have carried a large raiding force—fifty to sixty men—on a fast journey. Boats very much like it were probably used by the Danes in the eleventh century when they repeatedly raided the English coast. Although less than a quarter of this large hull survived, it was apparently built entirely of oak, making it very strong and at the same time, relatively light.

The second warship, fifty-nine feet long and eight feet wide, was built mostly of oak, but its three top planks were cut from ash. Scholars thus believe it represents a raiding vessel known as an *aesc,* the Old English word for ash.

The fifth wreck recovered from the site cannot be so easily identified. In fact, no one can agree on its purpose. The smallest in the collection, thirty-nine feet long and eight feet wide, the boat's sides were very low, too low for conventional rowing and too low to venture into rough water. Yet the hull was stoutly built, suggesting that it was used to carry heavy cargo. No other boat like it has been found, and there is no mention of such a boat in any Viking records.

It may have been a ferry boat on some sheltered fjord or river. Or it might have been used for fishing in calm water. But these are just guesses. All we can say with assurance is that its ultimate purpose was to carry a cargo of rock with four other vessels to the bottom of Roskilde Fjord to block the entry of an unknown enemy.

Chapter Twelve

~~~~~~

The Wrath
of God

Port Royal had more of everything—more beauty, more
wealth, more commerce, and more unvarnished sin than
any other city of the New World.

Most of the seamen who took haven in her well-defended harbor were pirates or smugglers. At times it
seemed that half the women who crowded her streets were
prostitutes and half the men skillful pickpockets. Every
other building housed a grog shop or a gambling den.
Most shopkeepers dealt in stolen goods. Warehouses
bulged with loot and contraband.

Sober citizens often said that an impatient God would
one day take vengeance on the sinful town. And when
the violent end came on June 7, 1692, it did indeed seem
that the wrath of God had fallen on Port Royal.

When the first jolt hit, the Reverend Emanuel Heath, rector of St. Paul's Church, was about to sit down to a glass of wormwood wine with his friend, John White, acting governor of Jamaica.

"Lord, sir," the minister said, clutching the table. "What is this?"

"It is an earthquake," White replied. "Be not afraid. It will soon be over."

But stronger jolts followed and the two friends dashed into the street just in time to escape a living burial beneath the walls of Heath's home. And Heath survived to describe the destruction of his beloved city: "In the space of three minutes . . . Port Royal, the fairest town of all the English plantations, the best emporium and mart of this part of the world, exceeding in its riches, plentiful in all good things, was shaken and shattered to pieces, sunk into and covered, for the greater part, by the sea . . ."

Another survivor gave a more vivid account.

"The earth heaved and swayed like the rolling billows, and in many places the earth crack'd, open'd and shut, with a motion quick and fast . . . in some of these people were swallowed up, in others they were caught by the middle and pressed to death. . . . The whole was attended with . . . the noise of falling mountains in the distance, while the sky . . . was turned dull and reddish, like a glowing oven."

Whether divinely inspired or not, the destruction of Port Royal ended a brief but unusual period in the history of the New World. It began in 1655 when the English captured the island of Jamaica from the Spanish and established a well-defended harbor behind a sandspit that extended like an embracing arm from the island's southern coast.

Three forts were built. The guns of Fort Charles cov-

The remains of Fort Charles still stand at the end of the sand spit, but Forts James and Carlisle sank with much of the town in the area marked by the broken line.

ered the seaward approach to the harbor. Fort James, at the end of the sandspit, covered the harbor entrance, while Fort Carlisle protected the harbor itself. Behind the protection of these forts, the bustling community of Port Royal quickly grew and flourished. Docks and warehouses went up on the waterfront along with ships' stores, fish stalls, and taverns. On streets leading back from shore, impressive homes went up. Many buildings were three and four stories high. There was a church, a synagogue, many taverns, and many, many grog shops. Eventually, Port Royal had two thousand buildings and some eight thousand residents.

At first the main business was piracy. In most cases the pirates carried letters of marque from the British crown, which designated them privateers and authorized them to prey on ships and ports of the Spanish enemy. In wartime, the privateers worked hand in hand with the British navy in attacking the Spanish.

Port Royal reached its zenith of commercial importance during the reign of Henry Morgan, who won knighthood for his raids on Panama City and other Spanish ports. All the loot taken from ports and from Spanish ships came to Port Royal to be sold and shipped to England.

Business was brisk. The harbor behind the sandspit could shelter 500 ships, and under the protection of the forts, the ships could be refitted and overhauled in full safety. On shore there was ample entertainment, mostly of a wild and sinful nature, for the sailors.

But despite its sinful ways, Port Royal was a beautiful town. Its sun-drenched buildings lined the streets in neat rows, and every building had a vista, either of the sparkling sea to the south or of the tropical, green mountains of Jamaica to the north.

Residents could justly claim that Port Royal was both the prettiest as well as the busiest town of the New World.

Even after peace with Spain came in 1675, and the British outlawed piracy, the place continued to thrive on trade and smuggling. And she did not reform. Just before the end came she was described as "the world's wickedest town," inhabited by "a most ungodly, debauched people."

The fateful day dawned with clear skies and the rapid swell of tropical heat. Some twenty ships lay in port. Most floated at anchor, but a few stood at dockside, being unloaded by sweating stevedores. One ship, the frigate *Swan*, had been careened on the beach close to Fort Carlisle. Her crew was busy scraping barnacles from her bottom.

Idle sailors strolled along the waterfront on Thames Street. They passed between the busy docks and the king's warehouse, between Littleton's Tavern and Fort James, and then turned onto Fisher's Row to inspect fish stalls and watch fishermen repair their nets and turtle pens. Some strollers wandered inland on Queen Street, High

Street, or the intersecting Lime Street. Grog shops were already doing brisk business.

Mingled with the smell of brine and fish was the rich fragrance of cooking from taverns where the noonday meal was being prepared. It was a typical Jamaican day, but some survivors later recalled that they felt an expectant stillness in the air.

Disaster struck some minutes before noon. It began with a distant rumble that seemed to descend from the green mountains. When the sound grew to a roar, the town began to shake. Brick walls cracked and fell in a storm of dust. The earth split. Docks plunged beneath the sea. Thames Street and its shattered buildings followed the docks as cries of terror rose in awful chorus. With its bell clanging wildly, St. Paul's Church, steeple and all, crashed to the ground.

A few people fell to their knees, praying, but most ran, trying to escape the falling buildings and the chasms that opened without warning in the canting streets. Soldiers dashed from the forts as walls behind them crushed their hapless companions.

Then came the sea, rising in one huge wave to engulf the streets and flood the ruins. The wave lifted the frigate *Swan* and carried it into the town. Those who could cling to the vessel saved themselves, but many others perished. In all, some two thousand souls died. Port Royal was leveled, and two-thirds of it sank into the sea. Thames Street, Fisher's Row, Queen Street, High Street, and Lime Street and Fort James and Fort Carlisle had all vanished.

Port Royal was no more.

Most survivors left the area as fast as they could, but a few remained to build a humble village on the sandspit. Fishing and limited trade with neighboring islands kept the village going, but Port Royal never recaptured its pre-earthquake importance. Even after drifting sand rebuilt much of the spit that had been submerged, the town did not grow. It remained a forsaken village, all but forgotten.

Old documents and dusty history books preserved the story of Port Royal's grandeur, but even these records were largely ignored. Port Royal might have remained in obscurity to this day had it not been for the American inventor Edwin Link and his wife, Marion. Link, who had developed scores of electronic and aeronautic devices, including the famous Link Trainer for student pilots, had long shared his wife's interest in underwater archeology.

In 1956 the Links indulged their interest by sailing to Jamaica in a converted shrimp boat and searching for the submerged ruins of Port Royal.

The task proved more difficult than they imagined. Although the water off the present shoreline of the spit was no more than twenty to thirty feet deep, it was so murky that divers had to search more by touch than by sight. And sonar, at first, revealed a monotonously flat bottom with no hint of mounds or ridges that might mark ruins.

Oldtimers suggested that the Links search around Church Beacon, the offshore light that marked the entrance to the present day harbor. The beacon, it was believed, was close to the old shoreline of the sandspit, about where Fort James had stood.

Initial dives revealed nothing, but after some six feet of sand was dredged away, the Links found traces of a brick wall, perhaps the remains of Fort James that had guarded the entrance to the old harbor. Then after further dredging, they found and raised a cannon.

The discovery was encouraging, but the Links knew by now that their equipment was not adequate. They would have to make extensive improvements before they continued. So they headed home for New York, planning a new expedition.

The main thing needed for the task ahead was a better boat. Link designed her. She would be built of steel and be powered by twin diesels. The hull, ninety-one feet long, would have accommodations for twelve people. There would be a special diving compartment near the stern with a large port opening just above the waterline. There would be two large air compressors, one to fill diving tanks and the other to power an air lift with a ten-inch diameter. There would be a large water pump to give authority to water jets for clearing sand. And there would be electrical generators to run deck winches, pumps, and strong lights.

The control room would be equipped with all the latest gear, including radar, sonar, and an automatic pilot. Glass plates near the bow would make it possible to scan the sea bottom in clear water. There would also be water jets near the bow that would propel the ship sideways whenever it became necessary to adjust her position at a diving site.

It took two years to build and outfit the ship. The Links christened her *Sea Diver*. She was the first vessel ever designed especially for underwater archeology.

While waiting for *Sea Diver* to be finished, the Links worked hard to correct a serious deficiency of their first expedition—the lack of maps of old Port Royal. This required extensive research. They could find no pre-earthquake plan of the town, but by studying old descriptions, the landmarks shown in postearthquake maps, and modern surveys supplied by the Jamaican government, Link was able to draw a map that gave a good picture of how the town had been laid out.

Sea Diver, under the command of Captain P. V. H

Fort Royal was the first major test for Sea Diver, *a ship built specifically for underwater archeology.*

Weems, sailed for Jamaica in 1959. Weems, a retired Navy officer, had earned an international reputation as a navigator. He was the ideal man for the survey work ahead.

On her deck *Sea Diver* carried an auxiliary boat, *Reef Diver*. It would be an all-purpose craft, transporting divers and equipment, tending the air lift and water jets, and surveying the bottom with her portable sounding gear.

The map that Link had composed from many sources proved invaluable. On the first day of renewed work at Port Royal, engineer Curt Scott, the head diver, used *Reef Diver* and its sonar to locate the walls of Fort James almost exactly where the map indicated. The spot was buoyed, and then, using *Reef Diver* again, the ruins of Fort Carlisle were located and marked. Thames Street, with its docks, warehouses, and shops, had run between these two landmarks. And indeed, on a survey run between the forts, the sonar gear showed an uneven bottom with mounds marking the remains of several buildings.

Link decided that diving should begin at the largest of these mounds, what he assumed to be the remains of the king's warehouse. Captain Weems steered *Sea Diver* to position over the site. Then a barge was brought alongside and the air lift was lowered into position. When the compressor fired up and the big air lift began to spout sand and debris onto the deck of the barge, everyone expected that valuable relics would soon come into view. But it was not to be. A few pieces of pottery and bottles, all more recent than the seventeenth century, came up the tube—nothing more. A shift of the air lift a few yards more away from shore brought no better luck, and the divers could neither see nor feel anything of interest in the area.

It was decided to move the air lift to a new spot close to the east wall of Fort James, at about the place where the Links had raised the cannon three years before.

Immediately the air lift began spewing up pre-earthquake relics. Mixed with bricks, pieces of wall plaster, and roof tiles were broken dishes and bottles, flint chips, lumps of coal, animal bones, and pieces of smoking pipes made of white clay. Divers constantly stationed at the air lift intake recovered a long-handled ladle made of brass, pewter spoons, a pewter plate, and a perforated bowl that had probably been used to skim soup. There were also several globe-shaped bottles of greenish-black glass. They were onion bottles, commonly used for rum in the seventeenth century.

Before relocating the air lift again, Link sent down a diver with a metal detector to search out a promising spot. The detector gave a strong reading at a place just a few yards away, and it was a simple matter to reposition the lift. The new spot proved to be the site of an old kitchen.

A partially crushed, copper stew pot, one of the first relics brought up, contained beef bones and the remains of turtles. Then came an iron grill, fire-charred bricks, a grindstone, pewter spoons, pots, porringers, and platters. More onion bottles were recovered along with a pair of brass candlesticks, and a thick piece of glass, evidently used to smooth linen. Five pots, two of iron, two of brass, and a fifth of fired clay had been cemented together by sea crustations. Possibly they were all warming on the hearth when the earthquake struck.

Pieces of plaster from the kitchen walls showed the impression of woven twigs or wattle. Mendel Peterson, a specialist from the Smithsonian Institution, inspected the plaster and explained that the walls of the kitchen had been built against a base of twigs that were woven and tied together. The twigs had rotted away, but the plaster retained their impression.

From the great number of pots and other utensils found at the site it was clear that food had been prepared in large volume. This led to the conclusion that the kitchen had either been part of Fort James or of Littleton's Tavern, which stood across the street from the fort. In any case, it was a valuable discovery. No other dig had yielded so many artifacts from a seventeenth century kitchen.

Soon after excavation of the kitchen was finished, six divers on loan from the U.S. Navy's base at Charleston, North Carolina, joined the expedition. They helped complete the survey between Forts Carlisle and James. Then when every ruin had been marked with a buoy, the Navy divers searched inside the walls of Fort James, using a metal detector to hunt for another cannon.

After bringing up a variety of cannon balls but no cannon, the divers next turned their attention to the building east of the king's warehouse, near what had once been the customs dock. Two onion bottles, the first found that were still corked, came up from the new site. Link, eager to taste rum that had aged for more than 250 years, used a hypodermic needle to extract some of the liquid. His experience, however, was the same as Cousteau's had been at Grand Congloué. The stuff tasted horrible.

Onion bottles and clay pipes, by far the most common relics found among the ruins, showed that the people of Port Royal were great drinkers and smokers. But in addition to bottles and pipes, the dig at the customs dock site yielded metal parts of ships rigging, a balance scale and weights, sword grips, and knife and axe handles. The divers also brought up a twenty-foot-long ship's spar without fittings. The unused spar may have been part of the stock in a ship's chandlery, a store specializing in marine supplies.

The most puzzling find to come from the site was an iron swivel gun of a type that had long been out of use

Clay pipe and encrusted onion bottles, common Port Royal relics, gave evidence of the town's most popular recreation.

No one can yet explain the discovery of a fifteenth-century swivel gun in the ruins of a seventeenth-century port.

when Port Royal was destroyed. It dated back to the time of Columbus. Had it been a collector's prize possession or had it been displayed in a store window as a curiosity? No one could say.

The most remarkable find, probably of the whole expedition, was overlooked by the divers and came up through the air lift. Fortunately, Al Banasky, one of the Navy divers stationed at the top of the lift, saw a flash of metal in the mud and grabbed the object before it was lost. He held it up, grinning. It was a brass pocket watch.

Link worked for hours scraping away coral encrustations before he was able to open the back of the watch. Engraved inside, the name Paul Blodel, a well-known watchmaker of the seventeenth century, established that the watch was a relic of the earthquake. Later, X-ray examination of the face of the watch showed that the hands had stopped at seventeen minutes to twelve. Survivors had said that disaster struck some minutes before noon. The watch at last gave the exact time.

After ten weeks of survey and excavation, the Links ended their work at Port Royal. They knew that a wealth of artifacts remained beneath the bay, but the hurricane season was fast approaching and *Sea Diver* had other waters, including the Mediterranean Sea, to explore. Although they were reluctant to leave, the Links could be well satisfied with their achievements. They had recovered many valuable relics, and they had completed a survey that would be a good working guide for any expeditions that followed.

The next expedition to Port Royal was headed by Robert F. Marx, American diver and author. Marx went to Port Royal in 1965 at the request of the Jamaican government after it had recently given approval to a harbor expansion program. The government wanted Marx to excavate as much of the sunken city as possible before dredges destroyed the site.

As it worked out, the harbor expansion project never came to pass, but for all the two-and-a-half years that Marx and his divers devoted to excavation, they worked under a constant state of urgency. Marx worked ten and sometimes twelve hours a day underwater. He managed this with the recently invented Aquanaut, a floating tube that contains a small air compressor. The compressor, delivering air to the diver through a hose, made it unnecessary to use a bulky tank and unnecessary to surface frequently to replace the tank with a fresh one.

Thus extended dives were possible, but Marx was hampered as the Link expedition was by the murky water. It took him six months to map a 200-by-300-foot area along the old waterfront south of Fort James. He was also hampered by a tight budget. He had to do the mapping work alone, and when excavation finally began in May of 1966, his team was limited to no more than three paid divers and whatever volunteer help he could find.

But despite the limitations, the Marx expedition made great achievements. Divers found and excavated a meat market, a fish market, a druggist's shop, a cobbler's shop, a carpenter's shop, a silver and pewter worker's shop, a cook house, a warehouse stocked with dye wood, and a tavern. Divers also brought up relics from a ship that Marx identified as the frigate *Swan*.

Many fine specimens of pewter and silverware, including plates, porringers, and tankards, were salvaged. The divers also brought up the remains of a wooden chest that contained several silver pieces of eight. Marx concluded that the chest of Spanish coins came from a galleon that was wrecked two years before the earthquake.

Later the divers found a cache of more than two thousand silver coins, all remarkably well preserved and highly valued by collectors. Another valuable find, a large brass oil lamp, possibly had once hung in Port Royal's synagogue.

Most of the relics were found close to or under the fallen walls of buildings. The walls also hid some grisly remains, the bones of victims who had been trapped beneath collapsed buildings.

Despite the remarkable discoveries, Marx continued to work under a limited budget. He had to plead with the Jamaican government to provide experts to clean and preserve relics. Eventually, the specialists were provided by the United Nations. Later, his divers went on strike, and Marx could get them back to work only by cutting the daily diving schedule in half.

Finally, when news came in 1977 that the harbor expansion project had been dropped, Marx terminated his work. He needed time to catch up on the writing of his many reports about his finds at Port Royal.

There is still much more to discover. In his two-and-a-half years, Marx believes he excavated no more than five percent of the site. Thus Port Royal, the town that had more of everything, remains an archeological storehouse, with more seventeenth-century relics than any other site in the world. They are still waiting to be recovered.

Chapter Thirteen

~~~~~~~~~~~~

Spanish Treasure

On Sundays, when he was not excavating relics from Port Royal, Marx, his wife Nancy, and any volunteer divers they could enlist, crossed to St. Anne's Bay on the north side of Jamaica to look for the two oldest known ship-wrecks in the New World.

Actually, location of the two ships—*Capitana* and *Santiago*—was well documented. The description of their loss was given by the great explorer himself, Christopher Columbus. The ships were the last survivors of Columbus's fourth and final expedition to the New World, an expedition that began in April, 1502, and ended in June, 1503, when he was forced to run the sinking vessels on the beach and wait for rescue.

Two other ships in the expedition had earlier been abandoned because of worm damage to their hulls. *Capi-*

tana and *Santiago* had been kept afloat only through constant use of pumps. So by the time Columbus reached Jamaica, he knew there was no hope of sailing his vessels back to Spain. Loss of the ships, combined with lack of significant discovery in the voyage, so disheartened Columbus that he sickened and died soon after he and his men were rescued. But as always, he left a clear record of his venture.

In fact, by reading the record, historians were able to pinpoint the location of the ships within a few yards. But finding them was not easy. The hulls had settled into the soft mud of the bay and been covered by a four-century accumulation of sand.

Marx located a timber by probing the sand with a metal rod, but he could not be sure the timber had been part of a ship. Early in 1968, however, Marx received help from Dr. Harold Edgerton of the Massachusetts Institute of Technology. Dr. Edgerton had developed a sonar device that read echoes through sand and mud, and soon after the sonar was put to work in St. Anne's Bay, it picked up the outline of two objects that were clearly buried ships.

The find was particularly exciting because most of the hulls apparently remained intact. The mud had killed the troublesome ship worms and prevented other colonies of worms from reaching the wood. Marx lacked the resources to excavate the ships properly, and he knew he must establish the age of the ships in order to spark interest in a full-scale expedition. He asked Dr. George F. Bass for advice.

Dr. Bass suggested taking cores of the wreck, and he sent Marx the tool to do the job. It was difficult work pounding the corer through the sand and into the wood, but eventually, Marx and his crew raised some thirty

184 THE SEVEN SEAS

samples and sent them off to laboratories to be dated. The laboratory reports erased all doubt. These were indeed Columbus's ships.

Today it remains for a well-organized, fully equipped archeological expedition to excavate the hulls, preserve the wood, and reconstruct the ships where they can be seen and studied by generations to come. This work will be done only when the proper expedition is financed.

To date, most excavations of Spanish ships lost in the New World have not proceeded with scientific care. There is one reason for this—treasure.

Salvaging Spanish ships has become a business with huge profits for the excavators and their financial backers. Although the treasure hunters have brought up remarkable relics and generally cooperated with authorities in seeing that they are placed in museums that can guard and display them properly, the main goal is profit.

It is not an easy business. There is a great deal of luck involved. Some treasure hunters never do make the big find. They experience endless disappointment and frustration. Burt Webber, a Pennsylvania diver, struggled through seventeen years of failure before he located the command ship of a Mexican fleet that sank on Silver Shoals some eighty miles north of the Dominican Republic. *Nuestra Senora de la Limpia y Pura Concepción* went down in 1641 with a huge cargo of silver. Webber found the ship in 1978, and the treasure, which he and his backers will split with the Dominican Republic, has a value estimated in the tens of millions of dollars.

Excavating treasure ships along Florida's east coast, begun by amateurs soon after World War II, has become a life work for several divers who are now employed by the Real Eight Company. Kip Wagner, a contractor, formed the company after his discovery of Spanish coins on the beach led him to an offshore wreck. In all, twelve ships have now been discovered. They made up a fleet of Spanish ships that were driven ashore by a hurricane in the summer of 1715. The ships were loaded with gold and silver taken from New World mines and bound for Spain. In 1973, the value of treasure recovered was estimated at six-and-a-half million dollars, and officials of the Real Eight Company said at that time that it would take twenty more years to complete the salvage work.

Not many other treasure ships were as easily found or nearly as accessible. The search for *Atocha* gives a more typical example of the challenging difficulties and heart-break that a treasure hunter must face and overcome. In this case, the treasure seeker was a determined Californian, Mel Fisher. To begin the story of Fisher and the *Atocha*, we must go back to the summer of 1622.

The hurricane season was at its height when Lope Díaz de Armendariz, the Marquis of Cadereita, led his fleet out of Havana, Cuba, his last port of call in the New World, and headed for Spain. The fleet had earlier stopped at Panama and Cartagena to load gold, silver, dye stuff, and tobacco, but it had been delayed in reaching Cuba by many windless days. Delay meant a late departure from the Caribbean, with the threat of a hurricane striking without warning at any moment. The fleet sailed under the protection of three guard ships, the *Santa Margarita*, the *Nuestra Senora del Rosario*, and the *Nuestra Senora de Atocha*. All three were heavily armed, but they also carried treasure. In fact, because of their protective guns, they carried the most valued cargoes.

The fleet left Havana on September 4, and despite the late departure, the marquis was encouraged by the weather. He reported "a serene and clear sky and an agreeable wind." But below the southern horizon, a brief but fierce storm was brewing.

The marquis, however, did not know this as he looked his fleet over with confidence and pride. He certainly had a right to feel proud. From his deck he could see some of the mightiest, most richly laden, best equipped, and best armed galleons in the world. And the *Atocha* was the best ship in the fleet.

She had been built in Havana specifically for the Caribbean trade. She carried twenty bronze cannons, sixty muskets, and a full supply of shot and powder. Aboard were eighty-two soldiers, and her crew of 133 included eighteen expert gunners. Her registered cargo included 901 silver bars, 161 gold disks and bars, and some 255,000 silver coins. In addition, there was the usual contraband cargo, carried by individual officers and passengers, who would deliver their hordes secretly in Spain to avoid paying the king's tax.

Although the *Santa Margarita* had the honor of carrying Don Francisco de la Hoz, the governor of Venezuela, the *Atocha,* as flagship of the fleet, had the most impressive passenger list. Among her forty-eight passengers were four Augustinian friars, including King Philip IV's special inspector of Peru. There were also several wealthy merchants from Peru along with Martín de Salgado, the secretary of the Peruvian Court of Appeals. Many of these dignitaries had wives and children with them.

On Monday, September 5, the fleet entered the Straits of Florida to pick up the strong, east-running currents that would help speed the boats past the Florida Keys. But before the fleet reached the low islands, the weather began to turn ugly. Soon, a northeast wind was kicking up such high seas that the ships had difficulty holding course. Finally, with the ships pounding and spray flying, the marquis signaled for the ships to turn, run for open water, and get themselves well clear of the keys. But for some ships, the marquis made his decision too late. The storm had already reduced visibility so that many captains did not see the signal, and even if they had, their ships were in such distress that they would not have been able to follow the order. Masts split and fell over the side in a hopeless tangle of sails and rigging. Rudders broke, leaving the ships to drift at the storm's mercy. And then, the wind took an abrupt shift, howling out of the south and pressing the fleet toward the very islands that the marquis was trying to avoid.

Although some ships in the fleet had managed to work clear of land before the wind shifted, eight were caught with no hope. Those doomed included *Santa Margarita, Rosario,* and *Atocha.*

The *Santa Margarita,* with her foresail blown away, and her mainmast and tiller broken, drifted steadily northward through the night as crewmen and passengers knelt on the deck in prayer.

Soon after September 6 dawned, the ship was swept over a reef. She dropped her anchors, but they found no hold in the loose sand. The *Santa Margarita* struck fast on a second reef. She heeled far over as the seas pounded her.

Clinging to the rail, Captain Bernardino de Lugo, commander of the ship's soldiers, saw the *Atocha* in distress about three miles to the east. Stripped of all but her mizzenmast, she was being torn apart on a reef. And while de Lugo watched, the hull heeled into deep water and abruptly sank without a trace. It was seven o'clock in the morning.

Soon, the *Santa Margarita* began to break up. De Lugo grabbed a spar and floated free of the wreckage to become one of the ship's sixty-seven survivors. One hundred and twenty-seven other souls on the *Santa Margarita* drowned.

The death toll on the *Atocha* was much worse. Of the 265 aboard, just five people, two slaves, two ship's boys, and a seaman, survived to tell how the ship had crunched across a reef and then plummeted into deep water.

Those on the *Rosario* had been lucky. Although their ship was stranded on a sandbank, all managed to get off safely onto the Dry Tortugas where they were rescued soon after the storm. But scattered eastward across some fifty miles, seven other ships had all but vanished. When calm returned and the flat sea once again shimmered in the late summer sun it was hard to believe that an immense tragedy had occurred, that 550 people had drowned, and that a treasure valued at more than three hundred million dollars had been lost.

Sailing to the area a few days after the hurricane, Captain Bartolomé Lopez came upon the stub of a mast showing above the water. When he worked close to it, the captain and his men could see the form of a large galleon submerged in fifty-five feet of water. It was the *Atocha*.

A floating chest, found nearby, was pulled aboard. It contained a cache of gold and silver, but it proved to have been the property of the silvermaster who had gone down with the *Santa Margarita*.

Soon after the *Rosario*'s passengers and crew were rescued, the Spanish sent Captain Gaspar de Vargas from Havana to begin salvaging cargo. He found the submerged *Atocha,* but her hatches were sealed, making it difficult for free-swimming divers to get at the cargo. De Vargas raised two cannons and then went on to salvage the more accessible *Rosario.* Another hurricane drove him to shelter, and when he returned to the area, he found that the *Atocha* had broken up leaving only scattered wreckage.

With the help of slave pearl divers, de Vargas managed to recover just a few remnants of the *Atocha*—nothing more.

No further salvage was attempted until 1626, four years after the disaster, when the Spanish sent an expedition to the area headed by Francisco Nuñez Milián, an inventive and daring leader. In Havana, he designed and had cast a 680-pound bronze diving bell to be used both as a search vehicle and a rest station for the pearl divers.

In the first season, the expedition managed to salvage 350 gold bars, thousands of coins, and several bronze cannons from the *Santa Margarita*. More treasure was salvaged in subsequent seasons. Divers, however, never found the *Atocha*, and after Milián died in 1644, salvage efforts dwindled. In time, the location of the wreck was forgotten.

So it was that when modern day, well-equipped divers began searching for the wrecks of Spanish treasure ships, attention centered not on the Atocha, but on other lost fleets, particularly the fleet that was wrecked on Florida's east coast in 1715.

Mel Fisher was first attracted to Florida by these wrecks. The owner of a diving shop and diving school in California, Fisher had already taken time off to search for treasure in Central America and in the Caribbean, but in 1963 he met Kip Wagner and decided to take a gamble. Fisher sold his California shop, moved to Florida, and put all his resources into a newly formed company, Salvage Divers, Inc. Working with Wagner, Fisher and his crew searched for wrecks of the 1715 fleet. All involved in the venture agreed to work a year without pay.

Before the year was up, they made a rich find, raising twenty-five hundred gold coins from one of the wrecks. Their success was due in large part to one of Fisher's inventions, a device he called a "mailbox." It was a metal enclosure that fit over his salvage boat's propeller to deflect the propwash downward while the boat was anchored over a site.

The original idea was to force clear surface water to the bottom in order to improve visibility for the divers, but it was soon discovered that the propwash could move sand. It was with his mailbox that Fisher uncovered the pocket of gold coins.

Treasure Salvagers worked with Wagner and his Real Eight Company until 1966 when recovery of treasure began to dwindle. Then Fisher decided to switch his attention to the Florida keys and search particularly for wrecks from the 1622 fleet. His interest had been sparked by the recent translation of a report on Milián's salvage work, a report that seemed to give a fairly precise location of the wrecks. It said that the *Atocha* and other treasure ships had been lost on the "west side of the last of the Matecumbe Keys next to the head of Martires off the Florida coast."

The report led Fisher into the waters off two small islands that make up the upper third of the Matecumbe chain. He and his crew, which now included his wife, Dolores, and four sons, searched the area in vain. Fisher would not give up. He continued searching for months, fascinated by the report that the *Atocha,* perhaps the richest ship in the fleet had vanished without a trace. But he was looking in the wrong place.

The error was not discovered until early in February, 1970, when historian Eugene Lyon, one of Fisher's friends, was working on his doctorate thesis in the Archives of the Indies in Seville, Spain. Lyon came upon a document that had not yet been translated. It had been written by Milián himself.

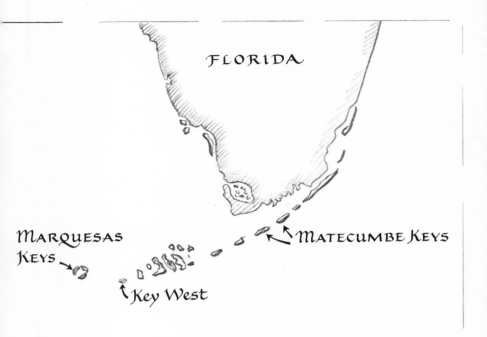

All Florida islands were once called the Matecumbes, a fact that misled treasure hunters until reports of early salvage work came to light.

Milián repeatedly referred to *Cayos de Marquez* as the island closest to the salvage area. The Marquesas Keys, as they are known today, lie some 100 miles southwest of the Keys of Matecumbe where Fisher had been searching. Lyon could not understand how such discrepancy in reports could happen until he studied old maps of Florida. He found that in the seventeenth century, the Spanish referred to all islands of the Florida Keys as the Matecumbe, a name that had since come to designate a small chain.

Lyon immediately wrote Fisher, describing the discovery, and Fisher lost no time in reacting. He moved his base of operations to Key West and on June 1, 1970, began searching the area to the west, surrounding Marquesas Keys. Meanwhile, he enlisted the help of Bob Holloway, another treasure hunter, who owned *Holly's Folly*, a well-equipped search vessel. Fisher and Holloway also

signed a salvage contract for the area with the State of
Florida, stipulating that a fourth of all salvage would go
to the state. The contract was later to be an immense
source of trouble and frustration.

As a first step, the searchers established an observa-
tion tower on a stranded tanker. Survey gear on the tower
could give the precise location for any contacts that *Holly's
Folly* might make with her trailing magnetometer, an instrument for measuring magnetic intensity. Then another
ship, the *Virgalona*, could be brought in with divers to
investigate the spot.

It was a good system, but the search area was vast.
Months passed. Hundreds of contacts were made, charted,
and investigated, but there was no sign of a Spanish
treasure ship. Eventually, the survey tower had to be relocated to cover an ever-expanding search area. Then,
after the tower had been relocated yet again, more information arrived from Seville. A special researcher whom
Lyon had hired to dig out further information of the 1622
fleet, found another account that said the *Atocha* had gone
down east of the last island of the Matecumbe. Fisher figured that this report would put the wreck somewhere to
the east of Marquesas. Again he shifted his search area.
But then, early in 1971, Lyon saw the original documents
and found that the researcher had made a mistake. The
ship had gone down west of the Marquesas as originally
reported. Fisher moved his fleet once more, back to the
old search area. It seemed that fate was hard at work
against him. But finally, on June 1, 1971, Fisher's persistence began to pay off.

Holly's Folly picked up a strong reading on the magnetometer, and after the *Virgalona* blasted the spot with
her propwash, divers found an old anchor, a musket ball,
three lengths of gold chain, and a silver coin.

The recovery was made in twenty-five feet of water at a spot known locally as the Quicksands. The depth matched reports on early *Santa Margarita* salvage work, and the anchor proved to be a type carried by the galleons. Divers continued bringing up relics—three swords, some matchlock muskets, several silver coins, and a gold coin that had been minted in Seville. Then, after the *Virgalona* blasted another crater in the sand, divers Rick Vaughan and Scott Barron shot to the surface shouting: "Gold! Gold!" Each diver held up a shining gold bar.

They were small bars about six inches long without any identifying marks. Gold and silver listed in galleon manifests usually had identifying marks that often gave the weight and karat value of the metal. Lyon, who had by now joined the expedition, concluded that the unmarked bars had been part of the ship's contraband cargo. In any case, they were no help in identifying the ship.

Strong winds ushered in the winter and forced Fisher to close down operations for the season, and when work resumed in 1972, results were disappointing. The season yielded just a few coins and some more muskets, and when it came to a close, Fisher decided that he needed more powerful sand blasters.

During the winter he bought and outfitted two Mississippi River tugboats, *Southwind* and *Northwind,* and rigged them with L-shaped tubes that could fit over their propellers and direct a powerful surge to the bottom. These two additions to the salvage fleet began to reap dividends as soon as the 1973 season began. By blasting out a chain of craters in the sea floor, the treasure hunters were able to follow a path of scattered artifacts. The path trailed away southwestward from the spot where the anchor had been recovered. The artifacts included iron and stone cannonballs, swords, muskets, and silver coins. Late in

Gold bars registered in the ship's manifest were stamped with seals and karat numbers. The Roman XXI and dot on this bar means that it is 21¼ karat gold.

May, the recovery of coins increased dramatically from thirty one day to 250 the next. Then divers brought up fifteen hundred coins in a single day of diving. They called the spot "the Bank of Spain."

The coins had been produced in the mints of Mexico City, Lima, Peru, and Potosi, Bolivia, but there was one eight real piece that bore the initials "NR" for Nuevo Rieno de Granada, present day Colombia. No other coin of the era from that mint has been found. It was a priceless discovery.

Other valuable and fascinating finds continued. Dirk Fisher came up beside the *Southwind* one day with a metal astrolabe, a forerunner of the sextant. It had been so well preserved by the sand that the numbers around the rim, giving the angle of star sightings, still showed clearly. Scholars have since found that the navigating device was made in Lisbon, Portugal, in about 1560 by one Lopo Homen.

Working back to a spot between the Bank of Spain and the site of the old anchor, divers found two gold bars and a gold disk that weighed four-and-a-half pounds.

On the Fourth of July, 1973, no holiday for the divers, they found a rosary made of gold, and coral beads with a gold cross attached. On the same day, divers exploring the bottom of the blown crater, brought up three silver ingots. The ingots were to give positive identification of the wreck at last because the numbers stamped on them checked with the manifest of *Nuestra Senora de Atocha*.

Mel Fisher had finally found his wreck.

But trouble and tragedy lay ahead. Fisher so far had been unable to sell any of the treasure because state and federal officials both claimed jurisdiction of the treasure site. This made it extremely difficult for Fisher to sell stock in his company and raise funds for continued work on the site. And then, partly because of shaky finances and partly due to rivalry from other treasure hunters, a complaint against Treasure Salvagers was filed before the Securities and Exchange Commission. This prompted a federal investigation that temporarily halted any further sale of stock in the company.

Tragedy struck first in August when an eleven-year-old boy, son of a visitor to the dig, went into the water near the *Southwind*'s stern while her propellers were blasting out a crater in the sand. Before anyone could reach the youth he was sucked into a propeller. He was rushed to Key West by helicopter, but he died just as he reached the hospital there.

So the 1973 season, despite the spectacular finds, ended with worry and deep sorrow. At the beginning of a new year, however, the financial problems seemed to lessen. The Securities and Exchange Commission closed its investigation after Fisher agreed to abide by all federal regulations on future stock sales in his company. Meanwhile, the long-standing boundary dispute between Florida and the federal government seemed to be close to resolution. The site of the treasure lay within the disputed area, but before waiting for a final ruling from the courts, the state and Fisher agreed to make the much delayed division.

The treasure, housed in state vaults at Tallahassee, was astounding. There were ten gold chains, two gold bars, a gold disk, and two rings. In addition to the astrolabe, there were three navigators' dividers. There were also three pewter plates, three silver spoons, a silver ewer, and a gold cup set with emeralds. There were eleven gold coins and 6,240 silver coins representing four different colonial mints. Forty-four swords, six daggers, and thirty-four muskets and harquebuses had been recovered. There were six stone cannonballs and 120 samples of cast-iron shot.

A gold boatswain's whistle was equipped with blades for cleaning the nails and a spoon for dewaxing the ears.

The divison of the treasure finally took place on March 2, 1975, but shortly after this event, the United States Supreme Court ruled that the site of the wreck was within federal, not state boundaries. This placed the treasure under federal jurisdiction and clouded Fisher's future claims.

But the 1975 diving season, Fisher's sixth in the Marquesas, yielded more treasure—more coins and three more gold bars. Working on the theory that *Atocha* had drifted into deeper water as she broke up, the divers finally tracked down nine cannons. The bronze weapons bore identification numbers confirming that they had been on *Atocha*. This clinched the identification and made Fisher and all his crew jubilant.

But then tragedy struck again. After leaving Key West, the *Northwind* had anchored for the night southwest of the Marquesas. Early in the morning of Sunday, July 20, 1975, while the eleven people on her slept, the ship sprung a leak. Then with little warning, she listed with a lurch and capsized. Eight people were thrown free, but three, crewman Rick Gage, and Dirk Fisher and his wife, Angel, drowned inside the boat.

It was a devastating blow. Heartbroken, Mel and Dolores Fisher discussed the future. Should they abandon their search for treasure? No. It had become their life

The Northwind, *one of the tugs used to blast craters in the sand, capsized and sank with three of her crew.*

work, and they decided that Rick, Dirk, and Angel would not have wanted their deaths to halt the quest for *Atocha's* treasure.

Fisher and his crew pressed on, more determined than ever to find the bulk of the wreck. Today, their search continues. Although a 1979 estimate of the treasure recovered so far sets the value at twenty-four million dollars, Fisher believes that treasure worth some one hundred million still lies hidden beneath the sea near the Marquesas. His estimate is based on the *Atocha's* manifest, which lists 897 unrecovered silver bars weighing seventy-five pounds each, the bulk of which was carried in the midsection of the ship.

Fisher has recovered treasure from the bow and stern sections, but the midsection of *Atocha,* with its fabulous cargo, continues to elude him. In light of his endurance and determination, however, it seems a good bet Fisher will one day find it.

Obviously, the methods used by Fisher and fellow treasure hunters do not come close to the scientific techniques and the standards established by Dr. Bass and other professional archeologists. But there are two points that should be made in defense of the treasure seekers.

First, without their energy and resources it is likely that many of the wrecks we know of today would never have been found, let alone excavated. Universities and foundations, the traditional backers of archeological expeditions, do not have funds to risk in long and sometimes futile searches.

Secondly, when dealing with Spanish galleons, there is very little that we don't already know about them. The Spanish during the period of conquest and colonization of the New World were such careful record keepers and chroniclers that there are few other periods in history that have been so well documented. It is not likely that the scientific excavation of a Spanish galleon is going to add startling, new information to our knowledge of the era.

But despite these points, the demand has grown for more care in excavating the treasure ships. Responding to this demand, the State of Louisiana has put its own restrictions on an eighteenth century wreck found off its coast by a shrimp fisherman in 1980. As usual, the finder will receive three-fourths of the treasure with one-fourth going to the state, but in this case, Louisiana will retain full control over the excavation, making sure it is conducted under the respected standards now well established for underwater archeology.

In keeping with these standards, the full weight of earlier experience, the latest methods and techniques, and the best men and women in their specialties will make sure that nothing is overlooked that might bring us new appreciation and understanding of the past. What more can we ask of any archeological venture?

BIBLIOGRAPHY

ANDREWS, E. WYLLYS. "Dzibilchaltun: Lost City of the Maya." Washington, D.C., *National Geographic,* January, 1959.

BASS, GEORGE F. *Archeology Underwater.* New York, Frederick A. Praeger, 1966.

————. *A History of Seafaring Based on Underwater Archaeology.* New York, Walker, 1972.

————. *Archaeology Beneath the Sea.* New York, Walker, 1975.

————. *Glass Treasure from the Aegean.* Washington, D.C., *National Geographic,* June, 1978.

BOCQUET, AIMÉ. "Lake Bottom Archaeology." New York, *Scientific American,* February, 1979.

BURGESS, ROBERT F., "The Guns of Atocha." San Francisco, *Oceans,* September, 1977.

DE BORHEGYI, SUZANNE. *Ships, Shoals and Amphoras.* Toronto, Holt, Rinehart and Winston, 1961.

LINDER, ELISHA, AND RABAN, AVNER. *Introducing Underwater Archaeology,* Minneapolis, Lerner Publications, 1976.

LINK, MARION CLAYTON, "Exploring the Drowned City of Port Royal." Washington, D.C., *National Geographic,* February, 1960.

LYON, EUGENE, "The Trouble with Treasure." Washington, D.C., *National Geographic,* June, 1976.

MARDEN, LUIS. "Up from the Well of Time." Washington, D.C., *National Geographic,* January, 1959.

MARX, ROBERT F. *The Lure of Sunken Treasure.* New York, David McKay, 1973.

MICHAUD, STEPHEN G. "He Dives after Cargo Long Asleep in Ocean Deep." Washington, D.C., *Smithsonian Magazine,* February, 1978.

NEWTON, JOHN G. "How We Found the Monitor." Washington, D.C., *National Geographic,* January, 1975.

PETERSON, MENDEL. *History Under the Sea.* Alexander, VA, Mendel Peterson, 1973.

RACKL, HANNS-WOLF. *Diving into the Past.* New York, Charles Scribner's Sons, 1968.

SILVERBERG, ROBERT. *Sunken History.* Radnor, PA, Chilton Book Co., 1963.

STÉNUIT, ROBERT. "The Sunken Treasure of St. Helena." Washington, D.C., *National Geographic,* October, 1978.

SUTTON, HORACE. "The Underwater Archaeologists." New York, *Saturday Review,* January 6, 1979.

THROCKMORTON, PETER. "Thirty-Three Centuries Under the Sea." Washington, D.C., *National Geographic,* May, 1960.

———. *Lost Ships,* Boston, Little Brown, 1964.

———. *Shipwrecks and Archaeology.* Boston, Little Brown, 1970.

———. *Diving for Treasure.* New York, Viking, 1977.

I N D E X